disclosures:

TEN FAMOUS MEN
REVEALED

Marian Christy

Publisher's Note

DISCLOSURES is not an authorized biographical work about any person. The text reflects the author's best recollections, knowledge and belief about the people and events depicted.

New River Press Web site is: www.newriverpress.com
Book Web site is: www.10famousmen.com

Cover by Francisco Rivera

FIRST EDITION

Library of Congress Control Number: 2007932977

ISBN: 978-1-891724-107

**Dedicated to the Memory
of Anna Christy, My Beloved Mother
and to Robert French, My Beloved**

Contents

Prologue

Thanks to long exposure to journalism, mine is a mind that does not bruise easily, no matter how great the insult."
-Russell Baker
author and retired New York Times *editorialist*

Extracting revealing quotes rich in content — quotes that enable a reader to glimpse what's masked, hidden or buried in the secret tomb of a man's inner life – is the foundation on which I built my world of words.

Now, for the first time, I'm spilling the beans, telling the dramatic details of what really happened on my jagged journey involving ten famous men. These are the untold secrets that had no place in the features and columns that I wrote for my newspaper. They still haunt me. To put them to paper, fashion them into a diary, lets you see the truth of me, the woman journalist facing up to ten men who cavorted across my stage.

Chauvinism thrived in my day. It still does. Like denim, it never dies.

When some famous men taunted me in-interview, when my natural female hysteria exploded in righteous indignation, I struggled to keep my feelings under wraps. I never wanted to be dead in the water. Not on my shift, mister.

Not all the boys were bad boys.

Fine gentlemen lurked among the rowdies and their miserable ways.

Once, I dissolved into tempestuous tears and was handed a box of tissues by an extraordinary man who stood by, silently, until I came to my senses.

That's the emotional me.

Once, I hugged a famous guy empathetically for telling me the awful medical truth about a recent surgery. And when he said go ahead, print it, I got sentimental.

That's the impetuous me.

Once, I apologized to a famous man I'd just met who yelled, literally, that I was a pain in the ass, to get lost, that my interview, and me, were a gross interference with his lunch break. I convinced him, from a smile, to let me stick around. He was surprised that a "she," asking questions and taking notes, turned out to be a pleasant companion.

That's the don't-give-up me.

I was a woman intent on talking to famous men, legends, about matters of the heart and soul. What I sought, and got, was the unsaid and, therefore, the unknown. He, any famous "he," usually preferred to conceal what he thought was none of my business. But that's the journalist's job: to reveal the unsaid secret, the unexpected *bon mot*, the real scoop.

There were other subliminal issues.

I always maintained a credible amount of eye contact. It was like, hey, she's not only taking notes, she's taking control. I did ask impossibly nosey questions. And, for heaven sake, I might be a woman whose pen was poisoned.

What man wouldn't be suspicious?

Some skirmishes became conflicts, something like psychological warfare. My best ammunition? My wits and a deep desire not to fail.

I was married to my career. And, just like a real marriage, the interview business had its ups and downs. One thing I know for sure: The ten famous *machos* in this book, with me in tow, gave war and peace a new meaning.

What people forget is that the interviewer is the other half of the story. What I brought to the interview encounter was me. My ideas. My thoughts. My concepts. My experiences. My opinions. My curiosity. Everything that was me. The famous men I interviewed did the same thing. The co-mingling of these very human elements are the dynamics of this book.

Conducting an interview is an awful lot like conducting your life.

We meet new people. We try to figure out what makes the other person tick or, heaven help us, ticked off. In the interview world, it's exactly the same. Only much more intense, dramatic, fiercer. Nobody famous wants a stranger to poke around his soul and print the results.

One big plus remained in my favor: The famous meet the press when they have something to sell — a movie, a Broadway show, a television special, a book. Their need was my foot in the door.

Here's the rub. They wanted to talk self-promotion. I wanted to talk self. Once I stepped from my newspaper into their arena, I crossed the threshold from the ordinary to an extraordinary series of *Alice in Wonderland* scenes.

Walk with me. See what I saw. Feel what I felt. Hear what I heard.

PBS superstar Bill Moyers, an old pal of President Lyndon Johnson, was one of the first men to stop the interview before it began. He shuffled some papers on his desk and harrumphed that he was too busy. Go away! He shot from his desk to the door. One hand twisted the knob. When the door swung open, his other hand swept into an out-you-go gesture.

This is what being shown the door really means.

I stood at the door, looked him in the eye, and spoke one word: ethics.

Moyers, an ordained minister, personified the meaning of "ethics." He didn't like that I'd dared to suggest that reneging on a confirmed interview wasn't ethical. A flash of anger raced across his eyes. It disappeared just as quickly. He invited me to sit down.

At the end of what turned out to be a fine interview, Moyers didn't apologize for nearly throwing me out. He didn't say thanks for the interesting conversation, or even extend an Edward R. Murrow goodbye-and-good-luck exit. He rattled off something far more brilliant, something that encapsulates the spirit, mood and heart of this book.

"They said Christopher Columbus didn't know where he was going or where he'd been, and that he didn't do it with his own money," Moyers observed as I was getting ready to leave his New York City office, my story in hand. "Journalism is a lot like that."

Marian Christy
Belmont, Massachusetts, 2007

Lord Snowdon

On playing games...

> **"I like nonsense.**
> **It awakens the brain cells.**
>
> *-Dr. Seuss*

One would assume that world-class British photographer Lord Snowdon, now the ex-husband of the late Princess Margaret, ex-brother-in-law to Her Majesty Queen Elizabeth, would not be prone to shifty behavior. After all, this modern-day Earl called Buckingham Palace "home."

Lord Snowdon's Boston domain, the one in which I was standing and staring, was hardly palatial. It was a small, worn-out room in the-then unrenovated original Ritz Carlton Hotel, now The Taj. Literally and figuratively, it was oceans apart from what I'd imagined to be his royal digs in London town.

What made the room stand out sharply in my inventory of immediate impressions was that it seemed too dowdy, too lowly, for a handsome gentleman, educated at Eton and Cambridge, a man so meticulously groomed and outfitted in a flawless, custom-made, navy blue suit.

Why wasn't he holding court upstairs in, say, the Presidential Suite?

Strange.

It took only one fast glance to sum up the total effect of his tiny cubicle. Old bruises and gouges in the furniture. Sun-faded blue drapes. Pleated taupe silk lampshade, dulled by time. Twin arm chairs and couch covered in clashing prints in dire need of reupholstering. What a tawdry place for Snowdon to hang out. The dingy details of that room were glued in my sphere of awareness.

Snowdon was standing at the window, gazing down at the floral charms of The Public Gardens. His back was to me. He spoke to the window when he said, "Come here, Miss."

Miss? I knew his name but he didn't know mine? Royal protocol is big on knowing the names of those who are in close encounter.

"Miss, look at the nice flower beds down there. Lovely, aren't they?"

Yes, I agreed, standing directly next to him, looking at the gardens. That's when I fell into his trap. He, still appearing to concentrate on the flowers down there, quickly asked a professional question.

"Do you plan to use a tape recorder?"

Me, nonchalantly, to the Lord: No, I will take notes.

Snowdon, nee Antony Armstrong-Jones, shuddered in barely disguised disgust.

He: "Why?"

I told him a tape recorder was a distraction. I didn't tell him that famous people held back, knowing that a whirring machine quoted them even when they stumbled, left ideas hanging and thoughts dangling in half sentences. I didn't tell him that my deadline was a few hours away. I didn't say there was no time to type out recorded contents and still do my job.

I wanted to say, "Trust me." Already, I know he didn't.

Instead, I shot back what I knew of his award-winning British television specials. That he, Snowdon, had painted the microphones black so that his subjects were less aware, or even forgetful, that everything they said was being recorded on a machine.

Snowdon continued to stare blankly at the gardens below.

Me: Don't you think that recorders (seen or disguised) can be distractions?

Snowdon gave me "the silent treatment" before becoming the ultimate con man. He said something vaguely uncomplimentary about note taking. "Doodles" he called them. Then he said what was really on this mind: Tape recorders have better memories than people. I knew, for sure, that my note-taking spelled trouble ahead. He also said he was "keen" on what he called the talent of "memory retention."

Suddenly, he swung around to face the room, insisted that I keep watching the flowers grow, and announced that he'd be "pleased" (pleased!) if I'd play a "game" (game!) with him.

The Lord, in the best of boys-will-be-boys tradition, explained the madness of his method. He'd ask questions involving the room's set-up and, judging from my answers, he'd gauge my ability to observe accurately. He was talking total recall. If I passed the test, he'd do the interview.

Ohmygod! I'm there to interview him on the basis that he's got a new book, *Stills*, I think it was called, and he's challenging me to a duel.

But what irked me then, and still does, is that although the fancy title, 1st Earl of Snowdon, was bestowed on him a year after he married Princess Margaret (1961), he was still media. Just like me! He was the chauvinist who'd shot fashion photos for *Vogue* and *Vanity Fair*. He was the chauvinist who'd worked as picture editor for *The London Sunday Times*. He'd even taken photographs of his sister-in-law Queen Elizabeth II and her husband, the Duke of Edinburgh, and, much later, Princess Di.

I knew why he was playing this stupid trick, this game, on a fellow journalist.

He is man. I am woman.

I only play games I think I can win.

The tiny room and its few contents were in a state of deterioration. That's what caught my eye in the first place. There wasn't a lot to remember. I never dreamt that the inconsequential information stored in my memory would be a prelude, and/or perhaps a deterrent, to my interview. I noticed things only because I thought Lord Snowdon, a man of title, would reside in a lofty spot worthy of *Architectural Digest* coverage.

I also knew that if his questions about the room were too exacting, my interview could go south. So I played trivial pursuit with Lord Snowdon, on his terms, still looking at the gardens, praying his questions would be shamelessly dumb. They were.

He: "On what wall is the fireplace?"

Me: On the left, as you enter the room. (Mind you, I'm looking out the window, talking to a piece of crystal-clean glass!)

He: "What is the subject of the painting above the fireplace?"

Me: Ye olde Boston. (I have a blurred image of a *Mayflower* madam spinning yarn!)

He: "Where is the settee placed in relation to the arm chair?"

She, realizing this was a trick question: No settee. Just a couch.

Lord Snowdon snickered.

He: "Where is the floor lamp?"

She, on trick question #2: There is no floor lamp. There's a lamp sitting on the end table.

He was shocked: Corrrrrect! I seemed to be errorless.

What Lord Snowdon, photographer extraordinaire, would come to think of my remarkable photographic memory was actually an accidental stroke of good luck. I'd passed muster. He turned around.

"Sit!" he said, pointing to an armchair. I noticed that his nails were manicured and colored the colorless way.

Snowdon's choice of the word "sit" was amusing because a photographic session, the making of a portrait, is called a sitting. Well a newspaper interview is a sitting too. We didn't sit face to face. Snowdon walked around the room, hands clasped behind his back. Sometimes he stopped and looked at me. Sometimes he didn't. I was snagging a good interview, and I didn't give a hoot that he walked and talked at the same time.

When it was over, when I had the interview in hand, I told him that there was an American version of his guessing game. I said it was called The Two-Way Street.

He narrowed his eyes to slits.

How about coming downstairs, taking a quick look at the Street Bar, turning around, facing the street window and letting me quiz *your* memory retention? I asked.

Lord Snowdon flicked his wrist in my direction. "A jest for a jest, eh?"

He smiled. His eyes did not.

No, I replied evenly, a test for a test.

That's when he stood up, his military posture worthy of a five-star general, shook my hand limply, said "call me Tony," and invited me to take tea with him at Buckingham Palace. He was serious. I gave him my business card. He asked me to mail him a clip of my piece, which I did.

He did not acquiesce to the test, coward.

Months later, when I was on assignment in London, I met Lord Snowdon on his home turf, his residence at Buckingham Palace. I was surprised that he seemed to be shunted to the back end of the splendid residence. His lodgings, at least the ones I saw, were more ordinary than opulent. The room exceeded the Ritz room – but only in size. This room had dusty, book-lined shelves with a threadbare Persian carpet. At least in Boston, the windows were clean. The palace windows were fogged. I got the distinct idea that he was not part of the Royals' inner circle. He was at home in drab, dreary surroundings.

An old man, a white-haired servant in a black suit, had announced me. Snowdon didn't rise to greet me. He just said "How doo you doo?"

I wanted to say: I did fine in Boston, didn't I, or I wouldn't be here, in the palace. But I just said: fine, thank you. Snowdon, wearing a sleek, double-breasted business suit with the perfect creamy shirt and dark silk tie, was sitting behind a huge antique desk, shuffling papers, pretending to look busy. He was doing nothing.

I sat where he invited me to sit. On a shabby tapestry chair that needed upholstering, on the opposite side of his enormous, very cluttered desk. This was the classic interview stance, face to face.

Only it wasn't an interview. It was tea time, in the office.

He shoved aside some papers, clearing a place for service. The same servant materialized out of nowhere. He poured tea from an ornate, antique silver urn. The china was fine bone. Almost transparent. The napkins were stiffly starched white linen, edged in a web of lace tatting.

The Royal Tea turned out to be tea only. No crumpets. It was austere.

Snowdon's background figured into the tea game. A great-grandfather, Linley Sambourne, was a cartoonist for *Punch* magazine. An uncle, Oliver Messel, was a theatrical costume and set designer. He was, in many ways, an ordinary guy, good looking, who sprang from artistic roots.

So there we were, Lord Snowdon and me, two press people with creative tendencies, sipping Earl Gray, lemon, no sugar, in Buckingham Palace. We were, basically, just two colleagues taking a tea break.

I suppose this was his way of saying "thank you" for my piece, which he never mentioned. We talked about the weather. That's the note on which the game ended.

Sylvester Stallone

On being Rocky...

**Things could have gone any way
at any point."**

-David McCullough, historian and author

We were floating in a dove-gray metal cocoon set on eight wheels. The stretch limousine was crawling aggressively, with amazing *chutzpah*, through a sea of ordinary vehicles moving with equal verve. The vehicle had sheer size on its side. It knocked deliberately past a taxi jockeying for the same lane space. The perfectly-timed shove was a close call, even by New York City standards. The shunted taxi driver exploded furiously, leaned on his horn and gave the blank-faced chauffeur "the finger" synchronized with the "f" word.

The chauffeur, gifted with distinctive cut-off expertise, glanced meaningfully into his rear view mirror and caught the eye of his world-famous client: Sylvester Stallone, a muscled gym god in a custom-cut, vested, gray flannel suit. The two men shared a split second grin of victory. It was the silent language of conquistadors.

Stallone's appreciation of the chauffeur's street sass was not unlike Rocky's knockout timing in the ring. Two men, caught in an exclusive moment of male bonding, imagine that combat is strictly a man's domain.

What do they know?

Stallone had already knocked me out of our original meeting place, his lavish suite at New York City's Sherry Netherlands Hotel. His publicist, who'd pre-arranged the interview, had set it up there. When I got to the fancy Hotel, when I asked to be connected to Stallone's room, the house telephone operator hesitated, asked my name, hesitated again, and advised that I hold on. She had a list of people who'd get connected to Stallone. She was checking it twice.

My initial fear, which I swallowed, was that Stallone had canceled. Superstars can, and often do, eliminate standing appointments, last minute, without a pang of conscience. That wasn't it. When the operator clicked back on, she told me to pick up a message at the concierge desk. The message was brief. Wait with the doorman, who'd advise me which limo was Stallone's.

Limo? This was the first time I'd heard of a limo. The interview was going to take place in a large, moving vehicle heading for an unknown destination?

Merde!

Oh well, this was no catastrophe. Correspondents descend into hellish war zones, drop into fox holes, chance booby traps and get their stories. I've scribbled readable notes in moving vehicles before. Abruptly slammed brakes and fast turns didn't stop me.

I'd interviewed the United States ambassador to the United Nations, Jeane Kirkpatrick, in a speeding limo weaving insanely in and out the fast lane from her New York City office to LaGuardia Airport. I was squashed, sardine-like, between several members of her security force, my audience.

Imelda Marcos, wife of the Philippines dictator — she of the infamous Shoes Scandal — fled a group of enraged Tufts University protestors by vacating the prestigious college premises. Suddenly things got scary. Campus police were holding protestors back. There were yelling death threats. Imelda hopped nimbly, Ferragamo spikes notwithstanding, into her limo.

I'd tailed her. A micro-minute before she closed the door, she invited me to tag along on her flight to Boston's Logan Airport. Again I managed an interview in a zooming limo, and got me a big story.

When I identified myself to the Sherry Netherlands Hotel doorman, he said he couldn't do anything until Stallone arrived on the scene. He flagged taxis. I waited in his shadow.

Sylvester Stallone eventually glided through the lobby door, slipped the doorman a wad that elicited a shocked, "Geez, thanks!", and stood silently as a tiger in repose. I introduced myself. When I extended my hand, his handshake, the texture of pure silk, was like the bare touch of a butterfly in flight. There was only the briefest of nods.

Suddenly, a sleek limo materialized and stopped where Stallone stood. The doorman opened the door with a bow and, after I slid in, Stallone followed. He still gave me scant notice. Stallone ordered the chauffeur to head for The Russian Tea Room, today a favorite of former President Bill Clinton. Without looking at me, Stallone announced that he had a luncheon reservation there.

Great.

It was a ridiculously short trek from the hotel to the restaurant. Stallone, then at the mountaintop of his *Rocky* career, couldn't simply walk there. He couldn't do anything without crowd interference. The limo finally slipped smoothly into a reserved parking space parallel to the restaurant entrance. Limos are a dime a dozen in the Big Apple. Nothing unusual. Hordes of nonchalant sidewalk strollers whooshed by, minding their own business.

Then all hell broke loose.

Someone in the crowd checked the limo occupant and went nuts with a shrill scream: "Rocky!" That "someone" drew a maddening crowd which quickly surrounded the sidewalk side of the limo. Pandemonium broke faster than a tsunami. Cadenced cries of "Rocky!" "Rocky!" "Rocky!" grew in tempo and tumult.

The limo was surrounded by people bunched together, glued to one another by sheer hysteria. If only Picasso were here to sketch the twisted faces, pressed against the windows. If only a television crew cruising around had stopped and recorded the sights and sounds of "hail to the movie king of the ring!"

Stallone sat as still as a statue, absorbing the adulation like a jabbed junkie. He'd invented Rocky. He'd spun Rocky out on paper, writing one of the greatest underdog stories of all times — a Philly flunky who, against all odds, punched his way to the heavyweight title.

Who knew that Stallone would be making *Rocky VI* in 2006?

Who'd have thought that the original film, which won three Oscars thirty years before, would land in the National Film Registry, a part of the Library of Congress?

At that moment, in the limo, Stallone's only thought was how to get safely into the restaurant. I favored a riot squad. Stallone decided to play Rocky in real life. He knew what all successful people know: A knockout thrives on surprise.

He struck his new, buttery soft suede Italian gloves rhythmically against his left palm like a miniature whip. His angular face, in the profile position, looked as if it belonged on a Roman coin.

Stallone communicated with the chauffeur via the rear view mirror. He rolled his eyes once in the general direction of the door on his side. The chauffeur hopped out, opened the door. Stallone emerged from the limo and....

Silence.

And the man's extraordinary get-outta-my-way posture was so powerful, the crowd froze – but not before making a path for him, just like the biblical parting of the waters. He stunned them without a stun gun. Nobody reached out to touch him. No autograph hunter materialized. No one dared. He displayed the raw Rocky iron confidence that lifted him out of the poverty of Hell's Kitchen, out of foster homes, out of delinquency, and away from an eccentric mother and an abusive father. This was Rocky out of the ring and into the restaurant.

The crowd dispersed quickly. I was still in the limo. The usual sounds of New York City moved in like a vigilant dragon, its cacophony intact.

When I walked into the restaurant and asked to be seated at Stallone's table, the manager stiffened. He demanded identification. I produced my press card. I locked glances with Stallone, just a few tables away. He, Adam, was seated on a banquette. I am Eve. He preferred that a she fight her way to him. The menu, large, was his front. He stared into the depths of it. A peachy ceiling light beamed down on him. He looked almost handsome.

Finally the manager waved a limp wrist in the general direction of Stallone.

I slid next to him. He'd already ordered a Caesar salad. I asked for a cup of black coffee. Strong. Hot. Now, please. Sustained by a few sips of caffeine, I spoke my mind.

Look, I said steadily to Stallone, you ditched me in the limo. Don't you know that fighters know no gender? I, a woman, work hard in a man's world. I understand the painful stuff of setbacks and comebacks and not getting back at all. A newspaper is one of the toughest, rottenest rings in which to be a winner. And that's the ring I come from.

Stallone listened intently. But when he stole a furtive sideward glance, a hint of menace shimmered through his eyes. Then and there I spilled the gist of what I wanted to know: Would he tell me about his life before Rocky?

His response was no response.

Will you talk about this? I asked. Nothing. I kept talking. Most successful men don't chat up their failures or flaws. Stallone crunched on his Caesar salad. I seemed to be talking to the wall. But I was sitting right next to Sylvester Stallone.

You beat enormous odds, I continued, even though your father beat the spirit right out of you. How did you get from battered boy to big-time classic movie hero?

Stallone used a smart tactic on me. He quoted a line from Robert Frost:

"We all dance around the ring and suppose,
But the answer sits in the middle and knows."

Translate that, he said, his voice slashed with condescension. Sly, as he is called, is sly. It was another man playing another game.

Stallone, like Snowdon, required evidence that a female journalist (who'd been a successful fashion editor and still dressed like one) had certain "discourse" abilities. I wasn't being quizzed on the room. I was being asked to interpret the allusions versed in a poem.

I took Stallone's bait. But on my terms. I interconnected my thoughts, ideas, into one sentence. I did not plan to repeat the sentence. I wanted to see how fast he grasped an idea from a she.

I leaned toward Stallone's ear: I am here, dancing around the ring of our interview, supposing there are many secrets hidden in your enormous success and, yes, the answers are sitting between us and only you know what they are.

"Are you angry?" Stallone asked. The walls between us began tumbling down.

Miffed, I answered.

"What do you know about self-confidence?" he purred in my ear.

It's built on underdog tenacity.

"Explain," Stallone said.

Confidence is a cumulative process. You connect the circuitous dots of small victories until it consolidates into the big one.

There is a point in every interview when the chasm of the great divide between two strangers in-interview slams shut. A thousand lights snapped on inside Stallone.

"I manufactured my self-confidence," he began. "I lied to myself. When I was fired as a mugger in Woody Allen's *Bananas*, that almost killed my confidence. It was a silent bit part. But, up to then, it was the most important role I'd ever played.

"Woody Allen said that my friend and me, we didn't look intimidating enough. I was crushed. But this kid with me, he was short, but he had tremendous confidence. And he's saying: 'C'mon, let's go back! Let's put Vaseline and mud on our faces, then look Woody Allen in the eye, act tough, get our jobs back!

"And I'm saying: 'Hey, forget it!' And he's dragging me back. Okay. So he does the talking. I don't say a word. And we get our jobs back!

"Now I'll never take 'no' for an answer. I told myself: 'If this kid can do it, no reason I can't do it.'"

Stallone blushed.

The hand that penned these powerful quotes trembled. Stallone had golden gloves. I had golden quotes.

Psychoanalysis. I dropped that one word casually.

"When I was real young, a doctor told my parents that I should be psychoanalyzed. I had to be tied to my crib with a rope. If I wasn't tied, I would get up and steal away. I wanted to run away even then, to do my own thing. I think it must be in my character, in my genes. Maybe it all came from my mother's frustrations...."

Your mother...I started to say. Stallone interrupted.

"She never had any real talent. My father was physical to a fault."

Your father... I started to say, and Stallone interrupted me again.

"By that I mean he interpreted his feelings by being violent. I didn't like being around my father. And my mother was so involved with my father that I had to be on my own."

On your own? I asked, trailing his last words.

"The first four years of my life, I lived with Mrs. Hanson. She ran an old-age home in a boarding house. I was a foster child. I never got along well with kids my own age. I felt unworthy. Yet, conversely, I wanted attention. I felt distant from my parents. And I had an overactive imagination. I never felt in sync. You know what I mean?"

Oh yes! I told Stallone exactly what I knew about being an outsider.

He was talking about not fitting in, being shoved to the fringe of things, the sidelines. I admitted to Sylvester Stallone that writing and painting were my two significant languages of expression. I called them my "voice."

The man nodded in agreement, said "Rocky" was his voice.

Now, looking back, I see that my confession was in the venue of those last-minute dramatic scenes in the fabulous *Law and Order SVU* television series. You know, when the clever New York City police detective, male or female, drops some extremely personal information in the lap of someone standing on the precipice of full disclosure. The crucial snippet of information, the detective's dare, is what gets the confession and closes the case.

He reacted exactly like that:

"I thought it was me, that I was an oddball," Stallone said, a note of sadness in his voice. "I was a delinquent. I was a truant. I was what you'd call a public nuisance. I was expelled from fourteen schools in twelve years. I became convinced that I was stupid. So I quit school. I became a beautician. That lasted six months."

Stallone, of his own volition, retreated to the biggest crisis of his grade school existence, which was an eerie forecast of his future, a Rocky in the making.

"When I was in the third grade, I had a fantasy. I thought I was Superboy. I wore red leotards and red shorts under my school clothes, and a barber's cape from my father's shop. I painted an 'S' on my sweatshirt. I was an emaciated kid. I had skinny legs. My friend Jimmy, I showed him my costume in the men's room – told him I was Superboy. So he told the teacher, and the teacher made me strip (to the costume) in front of the whole class. And there I was in my Superboy clothes, everyone laughing. It was cruel."

I didn't interrupt.

"It was the end of my fantasies until I saw Hercules in the movie. Then I wanted to be Hercules. Hercules was ethical and physical, a strong father figure. That's what I wanted to be as a man. I had Superboy in mind, and then Hercules, and eventually I envisioned Rocky. I created a character, Rocky, that was basically me, the way I wish I was."

I said that all ambitious people, men and women, reinvent themselves in their climb. He ignored the word "women." He talked only of a world where two men beat each other to a pulp. I accepted that. Women don't batter each other with boxing gloves unless they're boxers. They can knock you out with tongues that cut like knives.

"Boxing is the one sport where you're stripped bare of charades, put against another man who wants what you want – the prize. The humiliation factor of losing is enormous. There are hot lights, the audience a few feet away. And what's worse than being beaten physically, dropping to the canvas, and having a man with his arms raised in triumph standing over you?" What made you think you could be Rocky?

"The thought that I could do Rocky was blind, blind belief in myself. Many people said I couldn't do it. When people tell you the dream is impossible, you have to turn your ears off and turn your eyes inward. I pretended ignorance when people criticized me. Rather than debate, I said: 'You're right. I'm too short to play Rocky.'

"One person said: 'You're stupid. You can't play a part you've written.' I agreed. What I was doing was short circuiting my detractors. It didn't work. There's no smooth ride to the top, ever."

Stallone smiled sardonically.

"They wanted to buy the *Rocky* script from me. First they offered $75,000. Then $250,000. Then they went up to $360,000. If someone else had succeeded in *Rocky*, the stuff I'd written, I would have become unglued. It would have made me crazy. But I spent years developing *Rocky*, and no one was going to take that away from me."

He asked me if I ever had what they call a bad case of "the blues?" I told him I call it "The Blue Funk" and it doesn't go away in a day. Stallone pushed what was left of the Caesar salad away. His fists were clenched in his lap.

"I'd been feeling down for so long that it became a natural state. I had mastered, accepted, living on the bottom rung of the social strata. I was so depressed. I thought: I must keep on working…keep my mind functioning. If I'd adopted the attitude that opportunity would just come knocking on my door, I never would have succeeded. No. I kept on rewriting *Rocky*. I wrote it fifty times."

Quotes, quotes, quotes. Wonderful quotes.

"I could write on the subway. I always had a noisy environment where I lived. A real dump. I didn't know what solitary was. The bathroom was at the end of the hall. The subway was running by my window on an elevated rail. *Rocky* was my dream.

"The heart is everything. The heart functions as an anti-intellectual power. It doesn't know parameters. When you're emotional, you reach out, you participate in life. To rationalize things is to limit yourself. Go to any big city. You see thousands of beaten people walking around, people squashed by life. They have a common question written on their faces: 'Why the hell should I bother?' Very few people believe in the American Dream."

Stallone is an actor. He knew when to pause for effect. He made his words sound cocky, like he was playing lines straight out of *The Sopranos*.

"I believe in the American Dream. I set myself up with no options. It was either do or die. I decided it would be feast or famine. And what I wanted was feast."

Then he turned into Sylvester Stallone again:

"After I turned twenty eight, I came back to New York, and there was nothing for me. I wanted to goof off. But I'd say to myself, 'Remember, if you goof off today, it's one less day to achieve your goals.' I went to a thousand auditions. Nothing happened.

"The person I fear most is me. I always remember my defeats. If I'm tired, I say, 'Oh, to hell with it. Give it up.' Physically, I feel lackluster. Self-loathing sets in, and it can be destructive. But I face myself squarely and say, 'You realize you didn't put out 100 per cent.' And that's good. Fears keep me going."

Stallone smirked.

"Our confidence is an artificial state. It needs to be reinforced. Confidence stays strong only when the decisions you make are right. When your decisions are wrong, you can lose your confidence. But you have to kid yourself along. Fake it."

Nothing fake about Stallone. Nothing fake about the interview. He looked at his watch, stood up abruptly, left a wad with the manager and, before disappearing through the door, stood at attention and saluted me. He was gone before I could salute back.

This is my salute, Rocky.

Roger Clemens

On his mother...

**"Finding a new type of human being
and getting inside a new skin
is the finest sport I know."**

-Willa Cather, author

The rejections were always delivered on the telephone by a nameless woman who refused to identify herself, even by first name. I christened her Doom. Every time Doom's icy voice said "no," I knew it was doom for Roger Clemens and me to get together for an interview.

@#*#^!*#!!!!!

Every month, once a month for six months, I telephoned the Boston Red Sox office to request a Clemens interview. Doom, a woman whose tone was hung with permanent frost, took my calls.

"No!" she said outright, like there were no options. I assured Doom that I was flexible in terms of scheduling. I resorted to begging while trying not to sound too much like a beggar.

One miraculous day, when I put the old Clemens interview proposal to Doom anew, she relented. Doom rattled off a date, a time, a place.

I believed her. But only because I didn't want not to believe her. The Roger Clemens story was especially hot then.

Clemens, not yet a legendary New York Yankee, was the Red Sox superhero pitcher whom the sports press was beginning to hound. He was getting too arrogant, they whined. Not only that, some temperamental fans, swayed by the bad sports press, had shifted their bleacher cries from hoorays to hisses. Big league baseball, like any major sport, is tantamount to war. The enemy is any man who wants what you want: a win.

Roger Clemens was tottering on his pedestal, doing battle with his constituency, his image, his reputation.

Maybe I could break the tension if I broke the story in Roger Clemens's voice, how he saw himself, the man, facing an image gone slightly awry. I wanted to understand the source of his strength. Contempt swirled around him. How did he stay strong, focused, forceful?

Perfect timing for me, this big story, if the interview was for real.

I was getting ready to leave the newspaper, photographer in tow, when Doom called with bad news. No Clemens interview. A last-second cancellation. I asked why the pitcher with the golden arm wasn't honoring our hour together? Sarcasm laced through Doom's voice. Roger Clemens wasn't interested in talking to a woman who wasn't a sportswriter, she shot back.

I kept Doom on the line. I wasn't going to write a sports story. (The only thing I know about baseball guys is that they're physically perfect people who spit a lot, which is obnoxious, especially in television close-ups.)

Doom's "no" became more adamant, loud, when I said I'd like to talk to Roger Clemens about his days playing Little League Baseball. She was dangling on the edge of a tantrum.

I remember asking Doom if she'd reschedule, even "pencil" me in on another day, implying that there are erasers at the ends of pencils, and I wouldn't hold her to it, ha-ha.

She hung up. But not before telling me this was a hang-up.

It was so maddening, so frustrating that a pounding migraine hit me like a giant sledgehammer. I was this close to interviewing Clemens, and just when I thought I was sliding in, I was out.

Which is why I reached for my giant bottle of aspirin, half gone, and popped two. Still, if I know one true thing about the giddy world of newspapers, it's that things aren't always what they appear to be. Unpredictable office politics always changes things. The Red Sox office was no exception.

Who could foretell what happened next?

Maybe on that day, someone important was in Doom's office and overheard her frosty reaction to my last plea. Maybe that important someone asked Doom a few key questions. Like who was asking to do what? And why was it such a noisy "no"?

All I know for sure is this:

That very afternoon, the day of the awful Doom-induced migraine, I got a surprise telephone call from a woman with a dulcet voice who instructed me to meet Roger Clemens the next day in the Players Wives Lounge at Fenway Park in Boston.

What?

The Voice volunteered the word "exclusive."

Who are you?

The person sidestepped the key question. Which made me think that the call might be a practical joke. Your telephone number please? I asked hastily. The voice gave me a number. I scribbled it on the back of an envelope.

The voice said a "condition" was involved.

What kind of condition? I asked.

When the word "condition" pops up in an interview plan, there is always some sort of danger or compromise in the offing. The nice voice on the other end of the line said, simply, that Mrs. Clemens, Debbie, would be joining Mr. Clemens.

Double terrific!

When I put the phone in its cradle, a random thought hit me. I wonder if that voice was Debbie's, if she had taken it upon herself to set up a meeting. Had she been in Doom's office when I was deleted from her husband's schedule? Was she the type of wife who cared about the impact of a media brush-off? Was she Roger's best advisor?

Then another thought choked me.

Maybe this was a bad joke. And before you call me paranoid, let me tell you about my first experience with promising celebrity interviews that involved the telephone.

I was a cub reporter in a small, overcrowded regional office of a national news company, Fairchild Publications, where the cramped rows of desks put correspondents on a person-to-person basis. These were pre-cubical days. Nobody had any secrets.

A rising young theater critic, whose desk abutted mine, was

interviewing, at great length, Cher of Sonny and Cher fame. Only it turned out that the person on the other end of the line wasn't really Cher. It was a Cher sound-alike. Someone who'd been paid by an office charlatan with devious motives.

The charlatan-in-question wanted to be the theater critic, not a correspondent reporting dull, drab supermarket news. In other words, the supermarket correspondent wanted the critic's job. Instead of using a gun to murder his rival, he shot his colleague a dirty trick – this phony Cher on the line.

The ruse nearly worked.

The counterfeit Cher, probably high on something, started to giggle hysterically in the middle of the phony interview. That's how she blew her cover.

In the end, the critic laughed too. But not because what he'd just experienced was funny. He laughed in total relief, telling his office buddies he'd been the butt of a practical joke, and thank heaven the bubble had burst before "the interview" became a phony story under his by-line.

Pranks are common in the newspaper business.

What made me think the Clemens interview might be a setup was that the newspaper department I worked in, "Living," was around the corner from the sports department. Sportswriters there, many of them moonlighting as national television commentators, coveted an in-depth, personal Clemens interview as much as, or maybe more, than I did.

By now, one of them might have gotten wind of my long-term efforts to snag Clemens. Perhaps on a dare, and the promise of a free liquid lunch, one of the female clerks (usually attractive interns from Ivy League campuses) had picked up her telephone, got connected to me, and set up the Clemens "interview."

If this was the case, maybe the sports department was playing me for a fool. Maybe Debbie Clemens had nothing to do with this.

More aspirin.

But I acted as if I'd actually bagged a prestigious, Mr. and

Mrs. Roger Clemens interview. To boost my belief, I telephoned the number I'd been given by the interview arranger. It was, indeed, the Red Sox office. I confirmed the facts with a new voice, also nameless, who assured me that everything was "in order."

So, on the appointed day, I grabbed my notebook and sprinted toward Fenway Park. Wow, I was going to meet Roger Clemens and the missus!

There were a lot more nifty places in Boston to meet one of the baseball world's greatest pitchers, The Rocket, as he's known for the power and speed of his pitches. The Players Wives Lounge was a nondescript hideaway punctuated with a mishmash of Salvation Army furniture. It was the place where Red Sox wives/moms and their kids were hidden from the public when Daddy was on the field. Several old television sets blared replays highlighting the Red Sox game of-the-moment.

The kids had no entertainment. They entertained themselves.

One high-chair baby played ball with handfuls of ice cream flung haphazardly at older children who didn't duck fast enough. Unbridled kid energy is sobering, especially when they're playing cowboys and indians with a Ninja turtle. When the mass of kiddies shrieked or screamed, the room's decibel level zoomed into the red zone.

It was into this kiddie chaos that Roger Clemens, six-feet-four, strode with the absolute sureness of a Viking bent on victory. The room lit up with a thousand lights, namely Clemens's inner *klieg*.

In extreme close-up, Clemens emanated rock shock.

His blond hair was carefully spiked, sleeker than Rod Stewart's current look. He'd shaved real close. He smelled soap and water clean. Clemens didn't need a uniform to proclaim his masculinity. But he was wearing army camouflage like a soldier headed for a battlefield. His fatigues were ironed crisply, nary a wrinkle, and his combat boots, in which he'd painstakingly stuffed his pants, were shined to a fare-thee-well.

Clemens, a towering figure, told me right off that he'd picked this place on purpose.

"We're here," he announced, glancing at the Red Sox wives and children, "to check out the state of the surroundings. Dingy. Drab. Decrepit."

"Shabby Chic," is how he finally described the place.

The man didn't know how funny he sounded talking fashion because the pretty baseball wives and girlfriends in the room epitomized *Vogue* chic. They were gym lean and touting pricy couture-coiffure-cosmetics. Clemens wasn't checking out the women, he wanted this woman, me, to check out the room.

Clemens had, after all, angered his bosses by asking (demanding?) that the Wives Lounge be improved. Who was he, a mere mega star, to tell management what to do with their own property? The resentment he and the Red Sox management radiated was mutual and public.

What was none of my business had become my business.

Then I heard Roger Clemens utter something I would never have imagined coming from him. Baseball's *macho* man said that good women — the room was full of good women — never get treated right. Oh boy, I thought, this story, these words of praise for women-in-general coming from Roger Clemens... This is going to be hot.

Clemens talked feminism from a first-hand point of view, convincingly, like he knew what he was talking about.

"Women make homes and babies, but they're more than babysitters," he told me. "They're partners in the big scheme of things – like life."

Emancipation (that's what he called the Feminist Movement) had always been fought on the home front. Did I know that?

Yeah, I knew that. But how did Roger Clemens know that?

Get the picture of the drama unfolding:

Roger Clemens — twice a major league pitcher in the World Series, a Hall of Fame giant who'd eventually dominate baseball with 300 career wins and 4,000 strikeouts — was standing in the middle of that awful Red Sox Wives Lounge, telling me that great women, women like Bess, were the unheralded heroines of the world.

Bess? Who's Bess?

Ah, yes. A detail from my research popped into my brain. Bess was Roger Clemens's mom. The man wanted to talk about sacrifices good moms make, especially his good mom. I was on a home run.

Debbie, petite and very pretty, stood in her husband's shadow, absorbing his impromptu tribute to Bess, her mother-in-law. She'd introduced herself to me before he'd marched in and stolen the show. Instantly, I recognized her voice as the telephone voice. It was, I believe, Debbie's voice that made it possible for a "she" journalist to meet her man, who'd talk about the art of mothering.

So tell me about Bess.

Bess, just the sound of her name, Bess, was enough to call Clemens into action. He grabbed three chairs, two in one hand, one in the other, plunked them down, and said what I'd been dying to hear for six months.

"Let's talk."

Clemens was, at that moment, The New Man, the kind who lauds the value of a good woman manning the home front and, most importantly, manning the man, giving him her strength and backup.

I was surprised how loud a knell sounded when he contemplated Bess's passing.

"No one prepares you for death. When something happens to my mom, I won't handle that well. It makes me want to cry."

I never thought of Roger Clemens, he of the much-feared war face on the pitcher's mound, as a man prone to crying. At that moment, he almost did.

What else makes you cry?

"Sometimes I just cry inside. When I had a lot of trouble with my shoulder and my future seemed uncertain, I cried inside.

When my dog was hit by a car, I cried. When I went to my grandpa's funeral and I saw how his death affected my grandma, I cried."

As I write this, Bess is gone. She died in 2005. Emphysema and chronic bronchitis wore down her frail body. She was weak. She needed a wheelchair to get around. When she wasn't in the hospital fighting pneumonia, she was in the bleachers, somewhere, anywhere her son was pitching, sending him good vibes.

Everything that Roger Clemens is on the field, all his amazing strengths and ferocious fight, are his mother's legacy to him. What he is, she made him. That became clearer and clearer.

Bess did what most women of her generation rarely did, mainly because it was out of sync with times in which women endured bad marriages because "leaving," was tantamount to a disgrace. It had to do with that ancient, decrepit, death-do-us-part church pledge. Bess left Clemens's father, Bill, six weeks after Roger was born, taking her baby with her. Eventually, she married Woody Booher.

Roger Clemens was nine years old when his stepfather, the only father he ever knew and loved, died. He still rued the day Woody went to spirit.

"I'm a Christian. As a boy, we were solid churchgoers. After my stepfather died, I had doubts that God was fair. Why did God take him away?"

He wanted an answer.

"Why?" he repeated.

The death of a loved one is imponderable. It's always been impossible for me to either explain or justify death. A lingering shadow of sorrow flitted across Clemens's eyes, clouding them, when I said I couldn't offer an explanation for death because it made life seem so futile. I spoke what I knew of the impact of death: That it's the deepest of sorrows, the heaviest of burdens, the unbearable that must be borne. I told him I knew what the death of a loved one felt like.

Bess had played mother and father to Roger. The dual role was tough. Bess was tired. She was the mom who worked three jobs to keep her family together. She needed a crutch. Bess embraced cigarettes with an eagerness that's almost forgivable, except that they wrought havoc on her lungs. Even when she was sick, Bess was Roger's staunchest mentor. Even when the Little League coaches put him down, Bess softened the blow.

"When I was coming up, no one said that I was a natural," he told me.

"They never said that I was a can't-lose prospect. I didn't open everyone's eyes. They doubted my ability. I always had to overcome the doubts others had in me."

Bess, who goaded Roger out of the emotional dumps, reignited his fighting spirit. Her theory – and she hammered it home so often that it's still embedded in his brain — was that there's always a next time. She saw Baseball as a game of rivalry and revenge. It was Bess who urged her son to analyze what went wrong when he lost, and to fix it. She also reminded him that there was always another game, another chance to win.

"When I lose, I make no excuses. I face up to one thing. I pitched bad. It isn't that I was partying the night before, or drinking, or messing around. I pitched bad. Oh, that makes me mad."

The baseball world knows Clemens' "mad" face, frozen, even when he's winning.

Clemens has one special, indelible, emotionally-charged boyhood memory of Bess. He wanted me to see them together, Bess doing her third job of the day, stocking shelves after hours in a closed neighborhood grocery store. Clemens was giving Bess a hand. It was just the two of them, talking things out, bouncing philosophical ideas off each other. Bess was tired. But she was never too tired to talk Baseball to her son.

He asked Bess what she thought constituted the power to win. He didn't put it that way, exactly. He was too young. He asked Bess what would make him a champion.

Hers was not college textbook rhetoric. Bess, who always wore an apron in the kitchen, spoke from the wisdom of her church faith and her experience. The power to win, she told him, depends upon the mastery of using the power that lies within.

"I made myself thrive on that idea," Clemens said. Sometimes the Little League coaches weren't exactly encouraging.

"I decided to prove them, the doubters, wrong," he told me. "That's what got me into the big league level. That's what made me a power thrower."

The man was talking about himself – but everything important he was saying reverted back to Bess's enormous influence on him, her way of imbuing him with a sense of how to harness the force of his inner drive.

Bess saw every game her son played as being related to baseball.

"When I was a kid, I wrecked her house," Clemens told me. "She'd have everything set for dinner, and I'd yank the cushions off the couch and mess things up. I played war with my siblings." He was talking wild pillow fights. Bess believed when he was throwing pillows, he was imagining he was throwing balls. Now he even throws balls in his dreams.

"My wife, Debbie, likes to sleep curled up close to me. But my arms twitch. Even in my sleep, I'm doing pitches. Sometimes this wakes Debbie up.

"The day before the game, the night before the game, the day of the game…well, I growl. Debbie talks to me. I don't hear her. I watch television, but I'm not seeing. I'm thinking of the game."

It was Bess who bought him a large, door-hung mirror and urged him to practice pitching in front of it. That's when he started creating his familiar war face, the awesome one we still see when he's on the mound. Bess liked it. Never forget that reflection of you in the mirror, she'd said. Spook your rivals.

Who'd have thought that every big-league batter coming up against Clemens was actually facing "the face" that Bess wanted them to see? The I'm-gonna-get-you-face.

"The stares I give the batters aren't stares. I'm just concentrating on the guy who's standing sixty feet and six inches between me and my success. Maybe it appears that I'm making a face, that I'm looking down at the batter. I'm just concentrating."

Cameras love to zoom in on that face, show his signature game face. When I said that, Clemens grinned.

"On the field, I have to be cocky. I'm self-assured. I think I can go out on the field and strike anybody out. I study each guy in the lineup. I think of all the possibilities. I think of pitches. If I didn't feel that way, I wouldn't be in the big leagues," he told me. "Sure, the money is there for me. But being a winner has to do with self-pride," he said.

And what happens when you lose?

Heartbreak.

"I hate to lose. I want to force situations to go the way I want them to go. When I lose, I feel so badly, I can't go out and face the public. I pitch every fifth day. The four days after I lose are hard days. "I can get very frustrated," he admitted, "very angry. When I do, I just run, run, run. I don't like to stop. I push my body to the limit. Then I push it beyond the limit…after I run, when I'm so exhausted I feel numb, I go right to sleep. When I wake up, things seem better…

"My mom pointed out to me the other day that our relatives think that every fifth day I simply saunter onto the field and throw a ball."

Bess always told her son that baseball, or any great game of life, is nothing without a blessing, the acknowledgement that no one ever does anything great alone.

"I play ball on Sundays." Clemens said. "Twenty-five minutes before the game, I go to chapel. Some guys pray to win. I pray for health. And I give thanks."

Debbie Clemens interrupts to make a point.

Roger has a cherished video of her giving birth to one of their four sons. It's a treasure separate, worlds apart, from his Hall of Fame recognition or winning the coveted Cy Young Award six times — a record – or his champion image.

"Roger has a strong inner drive to win," Debbie told me. "Not just in baseball. But in life. He thinks of winning on all levels as a completion, as if he has come full circle."

That's what the baby video represents.

"He's not just interested in doing his best. He wants to be the best of the best. A champion has to have dedication and staying power. Roger is a champion."

I knew then that Debbie understood her husband as well as Bess understood her son. I also knew the interview was over. Mr. and Mrs. Clemens fell into a romantic clinch. They forgot where they were, the noise, the families, the blaring television sets. They forgot me. The state of the Lounge, the pivot of the interview, had no bearing on the moment. They were caught in a clinging kiss, the romantic kind. Oh, happy day!

As I write this, it's 2007. Who'd have guessed, in the wildest of impossible scenarios, that Roger Clemens, now 44, an extraordinary baseball legend, would sign to pitch for the New York Yankees again? His prorated salary? A cool $28 million. This reality caused Red Sox starting pitcher Curt Shilling to grump, "We don't need him."

I thought of Bess, wherever she is, smiling.

Anthony Quinn

On always being in control...

**Even skipping the subgroup of those well
known simply for being well known,
there are A-list celebrities who are
certified monsters and a lot more who are
public nincompoops.**

*-Actor Charlton Heston,
from his autobiography* **In the Arena**

I'm in the cave of a famous man.

Actually, it's a pricey, upscale, high-up, New York City apartment. But it's really a caveman's place.

The surreptitious, uniformed maid, smug, who'd opened the door to Anthony Quinn's apartment had an inscrutable, Mona Lisa face. She seemed as speechless as her Leonardo da Vinci double. Lips sealed and slightly curled up, to say nothing of those know-it-all eyes. This Mona Lisa cocked her head in the vague, follow-me language typical of hookers who frequent Left Bank street space.

Together we walked down a thickly-carpeted hall leading into a spacious, Old World sitting room. It took only a fast glance to know, at once, that something was awry.

The room looked as if a giant hand had sliced it in half.

The far side of the room was still intact. It had a cushy, brocade couch. Sturdy end tables. A couple of comfortable-looking armchairs. But the fine rug, real or imitation Aubusson, was rolled up to the room's half point.

The second half of the room, the one nearest the door where I'd been left standing by the vanished Mona Lisa, was nearly bare.

But it wasn't empty. On the wooden floor, with its high-gloss sheen, stood an expensive artist's easel. Anthony Quinn was abutting the easel that abutted the wall — his butt abutting me.

His backhanded gesture was tantamount to mooning with clothes on.

Quinn, apparently immobilized in the rear position, was as silent as his Mona Lisa gal pal. He was also a swarthy, stubborn saboteur who would not, under any circumstances, turn around. Sickening hordes of butterflies attacked my stomach like a swarm of locusts. I've always hated shunning. This was one of the worst kinds, professional.

I asked if we could sit together on the couch, there, to talk one-on-one, facing each other. Without turning around, he muttered something about this being his "studio." Anthony Quinn assumed, wrongly, that his arrogant back pose wasn't transparent to me, the newspaper intruder, a woman.

With his dry brush, Quinn dabbed no paint onto an already-finished dry oil canvas. The old canvas was just an ugly prop, a wild mish-mash of hardened, colored mud. This canvas looked as if it had just been pulled out of cold storage. Singer Tony Bennett, an extraordinary painter, has nothing to worry about. Quinn should have stuck to his day job. It won him two Oscars.

The dilemma.

In unrelenting mock concentration, Quinn fixed his face on the painting sitting on the easel, pretending to study it in mock concentration. No glance in my direction. Clearly he expected me to interview his rear. He said so without saying so.

I noticed two things.

He had a nice, tight butt.

And there wasn't a drop of splattered paint anywhere. Not on the shiny floor. Not on the pale walls. Not on the heavy drapes that started at the ceiling and flowed downward in a regal sweep.

This was no art studio. It was a theater of the absurd. This was no polite, professional interview. It was going to boil down to a battle of the sexes. Quinn's ruse was a stupid prank. We were alone. No one was there to corroborate my situation so…so he was on safe ground. Would a male journalist have accepted, and dealt, with the crazy actor's disrespect? Either the two men would have parted company huffily or punched each other out.

But Quinn was man. I am woman. Whatever punches I used to poke and prod him would have to be smart questions that were ladylike, civil, powerful. This would be a battle of words and wits.

Journalism, you see, is a genderless business. It is ruthless from many standpoints. Whenever something bad happened in an interview, the reporter was always to blame – even if she wasn't to blame. Editors of my time didn't accept explanations — "excuses" they were called — especially from ambitious women staffers.

That's the way it was. Editors wanted the story no matter what – not a woman griping about what got in the way of getting the story. Feminism was a young woman's protection…and I was a decade older than the youngest of them, a fact that put me in the old school *modus operandi*.

It was too damn bad that my photographer had been instructed to arrive in an hour, at the end of the interview. I needed the guy now to shoot a picture of the half-and-half room with its carved-out, phony "studio." I needed a picture of me, standing, trying to interview Anthony Quinn from his backside. I needed visual proof that I was caught in a web of fakery that seemed better suited to a Hollywood movie set.

That picture, worth far more than a thousand words, was never to be.

So I made some snap decisions. I'd write a comic column about the man's ass attitude. If my editor didn't like it, he could put it through the shredder. But I was dreaming. I'm telling this story for the first time; to you, here. But, still, I made mental notes. Real ones, too.

No legitimate artist goes to a real studio in a laundry-starched white smock and fine, gray flannel trousers underlined with spanking new, tasseled slip-ons that screamed Gucci. Painting is a dirty job. Working artists dress in splattered shirts and jeans. And then there was Quinn's nice manicure too. Too, too perfect.

I put all this to memory, for my story, however the story might turn out.

Quinn, who looked like "Zorba the Greek," was playing Van

Gogh (or should I say Gaugin?), holding his old palette in a one-arm lover's clinch. It was studded with gobs of paint as hard as rocks. Obviously the palette hadn't been used lately. Which explains the dry dabs.

This was a hastily-arranged stage set, on which the actor was acting like a painter, but not actually painting with paint. Quinn's delicate wrist strokes, the ones hitting the phony dried canvas, were wildly reminiscent of the *cordon bleu* system of breaking eggs. Think Audrey Hepburn, playing in the movie *Sabrina*, making an omelet the way she learned in an elite French culinary school.

The actor used farce. He was sure that I, a mere woman, wouldn't recognize a farce when I saw one. The charade, steeped in gender subservience, was on Quinn's mind. He thought women should know their place. If they didn't, he'd show them there was no such thing as equality.

Only now, as I relate this weird encounter to you, do I see Anthony Quinn's actions more comic than cunning. He was a cross between a tyrant and a toad. I also think it's hilarious that the word "easel" evolved from the Dutch word *ezel*, meaning "an ass" (as in donkey).

I didn't think it was funny then. At that moment, snared into this unique, ugly bind, I'm thinking: Oh man, I have to find a way around Quinn's easel and *ezel*.

This man was, I thought, emotionally-hollow, someone who was wildly manipulative with women. Apparently, he yearned for female respect, regardless of how badly he treated them. He thought female deference was his due. He had no idea that respect is earned, that it has to be mutual to have meaning.

There were so many stories out there about how brutally, and much too often, he beat his wife of thirty-one years, Iolande. She was a theatrical costume designer, a woman who yearned to maintain a semblance of her career. Quinn didn't like career women who put their careers first. He thought he came first, above everything, and that respect was his due, regardless of his *macho* behavior.

Quinn didn't have my respect. He had my attention. He was a 70 year-old man making a fool of himself. He wasn't going to make a fool of me.

That's when I dashed over to my briefcase, grabbed my hardcover notebook and pen, and slid to a stop a few feet beside him. We weren't exactly side-by-side. I stood at an awkward angle, so that I faced his famous silhouette. I hovered. Hovering can make people nervous. Quinn didn't flinch.

I jammed the notebook hard into my side so I could write notes without going wobbly. An interview, after all, is an investigation, a laser-beam look inside the man. Quotes. I had to get quotes. To get the talk ball rolling, I asked a direct question: I read that you were tongue-tied as a boy. How did you get from tongue trouble to being a famous actor?

Quinn's answer was shockingly separate from the question. He shouted a man's name, a strange name you might find in a Victorian novel set in France.

"Antoine!"

When he yelled, practically in my ear, I jumped. He used his voice like a stage actor addressing the last row of theater goers. The unexpected boom of his microphone voice at close range was immediately effective.

Antoine, who must have been waiting in the wings, materialized out of nowhere, like a puff of smelly smoke.

The androgynous teenager, a shorthaired ghost badly in need of a bath, was probably a for-hire acting student. Maybe Mona Lisa, the maid, was Antoine's wardrobe mistress. "Antoine" appeared as a Dickensian prototype street urchin.

His grayed, oversized shirt, complete with rips, was once white. His frayed cut-off shorts had been long chinos long ago. He had a bad case of acne. Some of the boils erupting on his face seemed about to burst their creamy poison. And he was wearing Max Factor pancake make-up, orange and noticeable. Antoine was, at least for the purpose of this interview, Quinn's hired slave, acting out his assigned role.

The Anthony Quinn farce began in earnest.

A little pre-interview research turned up some fascinating material on Anthony Quinn. For no reason I can prove, the stilted press releases I came across seemed to be make-believe press fodder. It read as if a Hollywood studio publicist of another era had dreamed up counterfeit media material to portray a rags-to-Hollywood-leap.

Quinn was born in a hut.

His mother was Mexican, his father an Irish-American soldier of fortune.

As a baby, he was smuggled out of his native Chihuahua, Mexico, to El Paso, Texas. The smuggling method involved his being stashed in the back of a coal wagon.

At five, the boy worked the streets, selling wooden sticks for wood stoves.

His parents became migrant workers. He quit school in the tenth grade. He was, in rapid succession, a fruit picker, a dress cutter, a taxi driver, a cement mixer, an amateur boxer.

Maybe this is all true? Maybe....

Then there's Quinn's amazing romantic history.

His first marital conquest was Katherine DeMille – daughter of Cecil B. DeMille, a big-shot director at Paramount Pictures. Reportedly, the straight-laced father-in-law, whose daddy was an Episcopalian minister, didn't like the volatile Quinn much. But, to please Katherine, DeMille snagged Quinn a long-term contact with Paramount. Which is how Quinn's acting career was launched.

Quinn had smarts. But it was his uncanny ability to control people and/or situations, subtly or flagrantly, that became his greatest skill.

He also had five wives. He produced thirteen children – the last coming in 1996, when Quinn was 81 and reportedly after he had serious heart surgery. The man's sexual prowess was amazing.

Allegedly, he kept three mistresses simultaneously. He attracted lovers in droves. One of his secretaries, Kathy Benvin, one of his paramours, produced two of his babies.

The woman who stood in Quinn's way the longest, the woman who irritated him the most, was Iolande, his wife of thirty-one years. One of their adult sons, Danny Quinn, alleged that his father had beaten his mother often, sometimes severely. Apparently, Quinn liked his women to fawn over him, to be subservient. He thought women were subordinate to men.

Iolande Quinn ran scared, literally.

Once, I happened to be seated next to her at a Rome fashion show given by Valentino, then Jackie Onassis's favorite designer. When I identified myself and asked her for an interview, her eyes widened in fear. She literally grabbed her belongings and zoomed off. Later, a media colleague from *People* magazine, a woman stationed in Rome, explained that Iolande was terrified that if she ever told the truth about Quinn, she'd get beaten – or worse.

In October 1996, Iolande quipped to *Time* magazine a few words that said it all.

"My husband think (sic) about the wife like a slave."

And there I was, in the caveman's apartment, with his current slave, Antoine. Or was it Antoinette? In those raggy, baggy clothes I couldn't really tell.

I decided to appear to cut Quinn a little slack. Intuitively, and only because I wanted him to understand that my manners were poles apart from his, I addressed him as Mr. Quinn. This time when I asked the same question, I sang his name softly, pretended that my voice was equipped with a taste of sugar.

Mr. Quinn, I read that you were tongue-tied as a boy. How did you get from tongue trouble to being a famous actor?

He shot back this:

"When I was a young man, I had a speech impediment. I really didn't know how bad it was. But then I designed a marketplace, entered the drawing in a contest, and won a scholarship to study with Frank Lloyd Wright. So I went to Mr. Wright to ask for a job. I was a poor kid. I was not dressed adequately.

All I had were patched-up clothes. But Mr. Wright didn't seem to mind."

Much to my astonishment, Quinn quickly referenced and, in a roundabout way, extended subtle applause for my use of the word "mister."

"I called him '*Mr.* Wright.' He called me '*Mr.* Quinn.'"

Quinn wanted me to see him in the bright light and major league of greatness. The first thing he did was to propel himself in the company of a genius: Frank Lloyd Wright, the legendary American architect who designed New York City's Guggenheim Museum, as well as futuristic private estates that have become architectural classics.

Antoine (Antoinette?) should have been cast by Rebecca Eaton, executive producer for PBS' *Masterpiece Theater* in one of her excellent Charles Dickens series. Antoine, the ragamuffin, flew back into the "studio" again. As it turned out, he was Quinn's fetcher.

With a guttural bark, etched in a menacing undertone, Quinn ordered the fetcher to bring him a tube of Cobalt Pale Blue. This color turned out to be one of many tubes tossed haphazardly into a series of corrugated cardboard boxes sitting in a far corner of the "studio."

The fetcher quivered in his rotting sneakers. He dug deeply. The tubes shifted around like sand. This was like trying to find a needle in a haystack. He brought Quinn a tube. I don't know if it was the right color. I only know that the tube wouldn't open. It was old. It was stuck. It was as dried as his palette and canvas. Quinn threw it on the ground, spoiled brat style.

That's when I noticed that the tube sported an X, via a magic marker. If another color had the X mark, it meant that Quinn went to great lengths to identify these props just like they do backstage. It was fairly easy for Antoine to find X-marked tubes among many unmarked tubes.

"Vermillion!" Quinn shrieked.

The fetcher went through the same ridiculous rummage routine and delivered a tube to Quinn. Sure enough, it was X-marked. And, as "Antoine" passed me, I got a wink. I winked back. Quinn, still in the back position, was oblivious to the tell-all wink signal. Now I knew that somebody else knew what I knew. This was an elaborate put-on, highly improbably slapstick passed off an "an interview."

Quinn dabbed vermillion on the dried canvas.

Mr. Quinn, please tell me more about Mr. Wright.

"Finally, he (Frank Lloyd Wright) said: 'You can draw. No question. But what's the matter with your speech?' I said: 'What do you mean?' And he said: 'It's atrocious.' Then he sat down and explained a few things. First, he said that an architect has to be a philosopher. He said that people lead horrendous lives, that they're programmed to accept anything, even tiny little boxes they call houses. He said that an architect has to talk convincingly, inspire people to live in new ways. Then he gave me the name of a surgeon. I had an expensive operation on my tongue, which Frank Lloyd Wright underwrote."

Then another yell. "Ocher!"

The tube, also X-marked, opened up.

So did Quinn. While he dabbed ocher on that messy canvas, he spoke.

"Mr. Wright told me I had to learn to use my voice. And he sent me to acting school. One day, I appeared in a play. He came to see me. This time he said: 'Why the hell do you want to be an architect? I think you should be an actor.' And I kept on saying, 'But Mr. Wright, I'll only be an actor to earn enough money to become an architect.' And he shook his head. 'Yes, of course,' he said. But he knew I'd never return to architecture. He knew."

The standout word "hell" in the quote amused me. I thought the cave I was in was hell. Mr. Quinn, I said facetiously, but with a straight face, serious, so he couldn't possibly read my thoughts: Do you think Mr. Wright was referring to the biblical hell, as in the big fire below, the place of the burning torture?

Quinn thought the question was, ahem, thought-provoking. "I don't think of hell as a possible hereafter," he replied. His tone was civil.

Well, Mr. Quinn, where does hell exist?

"In the here and now."

Mr. Quinn, do you mean that you look at interviews as a situation from hell?

"Ha-ha-ha-ha!"

Quinn's merry laugh had a melancholy undertone, as if it had been dunked in melodrama. I didn't laugh with him. I was as quiet as Mona Lisa, as distant as Antoine, who'd fled from the room while I was taking notes. Only then did Anthony Quinn turn his face around, just his face, to look at me. He asked my name. He almost smiled.

I asked: Is truth your quest? Is it what every artist, in every creative field, hopes to capture? Quinn returned his gaze to the canvas, tilted his chin upward and said something fabulous.

"I'm always looking for permanent truth. To me, truth is like a rock, something to rely on. The day I accepted there was a God, that was discovering a permanent truth. I had been involved in an extraordinary thing, feeling the presence of my father in the room. My father is dead. Only I don't believe in death. I think death is life continued on a different level. I once thought of studying for the priesthood. I had studied many religions but, in my heart, I never accepted the great energy and great power as God. When my father came to me from somewhere beyond, I bowed to a greater power."

Sometimes a journalist has to be a tactician. It seemed insane to be speaking of God, anyone's version of God, in the confines of this ridiculous stunt. But I did anyway.

I asked Anthony Quinn if he thought God was on his side?

"When I was nineteen, I wrote a forty-page thesis, a letter to myself, about what I'd like to be when I was sixty. I thought I had destroyed it. But not long ago, I found that paper among my possessions. I read it. And everything has come true. I had described the kind of house I would like to live in. The country. The types of friends I'd choose. I was amazed. I was actually living the life I had prognosticated for myself. It was as if I had a self vision, and God had made me into that person exactly."

Time was running out. My next question — coming in for the kill – was in narrative form.

Mr. Quinn, I said, God is synonymous with love. You've had quite a love life, miles apart from your love of God. You've had many wives. Many mistresses. Many women. You seem to me to be a contradiction in terms.

Anthony Quinn rose to the occasion. I almost forgave his absurd studio set-up. His rear stance, unchanged. The frivolous fetcher. The dumb painting act. I almost forgave him everything because, at last, he told the truth about himself. This is what I came for, what I wanted to hear about his women and his womanizing.

"My danger is that I tend to love in abstraction," he admitted. "I find it hard to love in particular. It's easy to love an audience. The only demand I make is: 'Enjoy!' But in one-on-one love, I make many demands. Love should be unconditional. I make conditions. I am not a good husband. To be a good husband, you have to subjugate your need to the needs of your mate. But marriage is like a poker game. It's a great gamble. You have to define the stakes."

And he didn't stop there.

"I have not lived an exemplary life. I am not perfect. I've often been driven by fears and insecurities. Usually I do interviews where I say the things that are expected of me. I am saying unorthodox things to you."

He paused. "This is the real me."

Quinn's admissions, floating around "the studio" like flashes of lightning, were shattered by Mona Lisa, who was followed by my photographer lugging expensive camera equipment, which immediately caught Quinn's fancy.

The interview quickly turned into, and ended, on a man-to-man note. Quinn disengaged himself from the easel freeze, threw off his "smock," and greeted his fellow man with a hearty hello, an affable handshake and friendly slap on the shoulder. The two men talked cameras, angles, lens, focus, shutter speed. Instead of being glued to the easel, Quinn was glued in front of the camera. He, in fact, directed the cameraman on the shot. He wanted to be seated in front of his awful painting. He wanted to pose this way – and did. Usually, photographers balk at being bossed. This one was putty in the hands of the ultimate controller. He did as he was told.

I exited as quietly as I'd entered, the echo of two contented men in respectful collaboration fading as I opened the door to let myself out.

Neither Mona Lisa nor Antoine was around. They'd finished their act and, I think, gone home.

James Earl Jones

On stuttering...

**"It is difficult to get the news from poems
Yet men die miserably every day for lack
Of what is found there"**
-William Carlos Williams, poet

In private reverie, when I skirmish with memorable moments of interviews with famous men, there's just one time, and to only one man, that I wish I'd spoken the language of poetry: James Earl Jones. In the actual interview, nothing rhymed. There were no iambics. No pentameters. No sonnets. Jones's spoken lyrics vibrated his own inner rhythms. He talked the way a poet talks, in ways that say the maximum with the minimum.

Like his take on the joy of absolute quiet between two people in love:

"Some of the best moments I have with my wife are when we don't feel a necessity to talk. We just sit in silence and do not feel separated. It's a reassuring feeling, a communion that goes beyond words."

How I wish I'd countered with what the poet Ben Jonson said on the same subject:

"In small proportions we just beauties see;

And in short measures life may perfect be."

Jones, who is a poet, happened to be dressed like one from another era. A snowy poet's shirt with puffy Shakespearian sleeves, topped by a brocade vest collared in velvet. The fact that his cuffed trousers melted past heavy workman's boots suggested that he, a gentleman, was always ready to soldier on, to do battle.

Jones had been touring colleges and universities, narrating the wondrous tales of traveling minstrels of past centuries. He told stories of minstrels who spoke poetry or, before poetry was put to paper, sang or chanted poetry. Jones knew much, and talked much, about Walt Whitman, Carl Sandburg and Robert Frost.

But the big reason I thought of poetry when I thought of Jones, was that for six years, from the age of eight to fourteen, years when impressions become ingrained, Jones, the poet, did not speak at all.

Six years of saying absolutely nothing to nobody.

One of his astute, caring teachers discovered Jones's poems. Read, for us, the teacher urged. Out loud. In class. Psychologists refer to the teacher's method as "forced public speaking." But the teacher's prodding was so gentle, so kind, that Jones stood tall, proud. The allure of reaching an audience with his voice, with a poem, was totally irresistible.

Jones, the boy, had no inkling that he was, for the first time, tapping his natural talent as an actor. Or that his voice, sound asleep for six years, would ultimately be his greatest tool.

When he started reading, it was as if his voice was being throttled awake. It was foggy. It shook. So did he. He'd mastered the poem in his brain. But, in mid-recitation, he stuttered. He ignored the flub. Continued. Worked around a bad moment. Improvised. But Jones told me that, in his heart, he felt as if his bubble had burst.

I wish I'd quoted W. Drummond to him then:

**This life, which seems so fair
Is like a bubble blown up in air...**

After Jones spoke of his first crucial stand-up-in-class reading, he asked me a question, boomed it in his unmistakable bass voice: "Did you know that some stutterers stomp their feet a lot in the great struggle to overcome stuttering?"

I didn't know that.

Anger and frustration probably figured into Jones's many stomps. Maybe even justifiable rage. So what? There's an old saying that something good can come out of something bad – if, big if, you look at "bad" as a lesson learned.

The disappointing day that Jones stuttered out of his shell of silence, he made two crucial resolutions. He decided to use his eyes more. To monopolize the sights of life playing out before him like a non-stop movie. He saw ordinary life happenings as scenes. He noticed details. The ways people acted and reacted to each other. How they spoke. What they spoke and what they really meant. He tuned into tones of voice, how the pitch of a voice changes the quality, and import, of the spoken word.

Jones, on his own, was beginning to absorb the raw rudiments of acting: "When I was not busy talking, I was busy observing," he told me simply. "I also built up my need to say what I really felt."

On that fateful day, Jones also made up his mind to pick and choose his words carefully. That was his beginning. To avoid words that might trip him up. Fancy, frilly, fussy unpronounceable words were banned from his vocabulary. Brevity, in the form of condensed wisdom, is what poetry is all about.

It was from these miniscule seeds, planted by Jones for his own emancipation, that led to his two Tonys. Four Emmys. Honorary degrees from Yale and Princeton.

From silence and stuttering came a stellar career built on what he'd kept locked inside: voice, enunciation, elocution, conviction that he could make the previously unworkable workable. A miracle.

How well I remember the residue of panic that pooled in Maya Angelou's eyes – she being one of America's most famous poet laureates – when she spoke of being a voluntary mute at age seven, after a vicious rape. She didn't say a word until she was twelve.

"I decided that my whole body was an ear," she'd revealed in our interview. "I said: 'I'll eat all the sounds of voices, the sounds of words, the sounds of song, all the sounds.' Silence can be good, in moderation. Silence is a way of dealing with things. People in various cultures meditate. Meditation is silence."

Was it like that for you? I asked Jones.

"I have one voice with which to communicate," he responded. "Sometimes I ramble. I rambled when I started talking again. I rambled, looking for the right words to say then. But I bet the average dog or cat owner wouldn't like the pet so much if the animal could shoot the breeze. Pets express themselves…but not in words."

I asked Jones if he was alluding, in a roundabout way, to the classic cliché: Actions speak louder than words.

"Yes," is all he said. His muteness was born of being inconsolable, after being deserted by the person he loved most. His father.

Jones, an only child, was born in Arkabutla, Mississippi.

Daddy, whom he adored, just up and left him one day, headed for New York City, aiming to be a stage actor. Jones, the boy, wasn't prepared for what he thought of as abandonment. Grief and disbelief whopped him. He couldn't fathom, or justify, his father's fast exit. He was just a child. Someone you love doesn't discard you without warning. The boy thought, somehow, that he was at fault.

Jones neither mentioned his father nor identified his mother.

All I knew, from a little research, was that his daddy had dumped him on a farm near Jackson, Michigan, where he was raised by his maternal grandparents — along with six other children.

"A Huck Finn kind of life," he said to me. He had recounted it before, in several interviews.

So scratch that quote. Jones and Huck had nothing in common.

Mark Twain's *The Adventures of Huckleberry Finn* was written in the first person. Huck narrated his own story, which automatically made him a big talker. Huck never walked alone. He was what we now call "a mixer," sociable and opinionated.

Jones and Huck had different boyhoods.

When Jones, the boy, walked, he was wrapped in the shroud of his own quiet — even when he was among other children who prattled among themselves, laughed and traded confidences.

Robert Frost wrote two stunning lines that capture Jones's early boyhood feelings of aloneness, even in a crowd:

I had for my winter evening walk
No one at all with whom to talk…

Jones, then fifty seven, spent years ruminating about the meaning of those six silent years. As he turned the situation over and over in the annals of his mind, he discovered the bright side of his imposed silence.

It made him acutely sensitive to everything and everyone. Closing off his voice had opened up his ability to see more, to be responsive and susceptible to feelings churning around him. It is that intense sensitivity, now honed to its keenest, that allowed Jones to take on other *personas*, different characters, and become the highly persuasive actor he is.

"I was shy as a child. Shy people are vulnerable. Shyness isn't bashfulness. Shyness is essentially vulnerability. The shyer the actor, the richer the actor"

Strangely, the late Richard Condon, the superb satirist and crime author who wrote *Prizzi's Honor*, also was fifty-seven years old when he talked to me about being a child stutterer. Condon's father, like Jones's father, was to blame.

"My father was a shouter. I retaliated by stuttering on purpose," Condon admitted. "There's a saying that infant fish swimming through the water receive most of their bruises from contact with parent fish. I believe that. You bet I do."

Condon added something startling, a confession, which in my mind further linked him to Jones.

"I finally made peace with him (his father) when I was fifty seven," Condon told me. "I no longer felt I needed revenge. I no longer considered him an adversary. Those days were gone forever."

Age fifty seven was a pivotal year for each man, a time of life when each man spoke to me separately, without embarrassment, about stuttering publicly.

Aristotle, the ancient Greek philosopher who wrote about everything, including drama and poetry, believed that tragedy was the highest inspiration for the expression of art. Aristotle thought that tragedy is a creative propeller. It makes you want to express what you feel, put it to words, get it out. Tragedy doesn't have to be of epic proportions. Tragedy is very personal. You feel your own sorrows more deeply, more profoundly, than anyone can imagine.

Condon:

"...Everything we do, all our responses, are rooted in the past. The things we learn when we are young are how we react as adults."

Jones:

"I was taught self-reliance very early. My grandparents brought me up. I was part of a large family. One of the benefits of not being an only child is that you learn survival.

"The lessons of survival turned out to be important. An actor gets rejected two to ten times a day. Doors have been slammed in my face. Not literally. I'm a big guy. But rejection is damaging. A big guy can be hurt. When I was rejected for a role, I said to myself: 'Maybe I was too tall or too black or too masculine.' That kind of reasoning has made it possible for me to accept rejection."

Walt Whitman wrote poetry that seemed tailor-made for both men:

Only themselves understand themselves
and the likes of themselves
As souls only understand souls.

Jones is known the world over as The Voice. Darth Vader of *Star Wars* was Jones's voice. The voice of Mufasa in *The Lion King* was Jones's too.

He's also been the voice of CNN and Verizon.

It's hard to imagine that The Voice had no voice as a young child. It's equally hard to imagine that he still gets a little nervous using that Voice, that there remains a tinge of insecurity in his soul. He never stutters publicly, or in performance, but he has not discarded stuttering as a dead issue.

"When I did voice-over commercials for a living, I found out that blood pressure rises when you're behind a microphone. Tension increases and affects the body. I found that curious. I suspect we were not always meant to be speaking beings. That knocks the hell out of show business, doesn't it?"

Later, as he became more famous, he taught himself to project both his voice and the feelings feeding the voice. Everything that he's ever held back, all the emotions locked inside his soul, he channeled into acting.

"Acting is a profession that puts you back into a state of dependence. I always hope the audience hears me. I hope they understand what I'm saying. It's easy to speak great soliloquies and not be heard.

"The idea behind the words has to connect to the listener's mind. The actor's responsibility has to be the conduit. Acting is a responsive art."

When I first met Jones, he looked at me askance.

This grand hulk of a man, with the build of the nightclub bouncer, asked that I be shut out, erased, from his sphere. He'd been on the set of a television taping of *Long Ago & Far Away*, a children's series being produced by PBS-Boston. He was tired. He'd been escorted from the set to someone's "office," a cubicle the size of a telephone booth.

He growled that I was an "interferer."

"Madam, you are infringing upon my lunch break," he said melodramatically.

The interview was set up by a PBS publicity person who, when Jones suggested I get lost, slunk out of the room like a scared cat. I asked Jones to please let me stay. I assured him I'd be no bother. I apologized for the bad timing. I told him that interviews over lunch weren't unusual. I asked if I could just keep him company while he ate. Okay?

"Okay," he mumbled.

But he didn't have a lunch hour, only thirty minutes. That meant my interview would have to move fast. Someone brought him a battered cafeteria tray. On it sat a stingy scoop of tuna on wilted lettuce. The slice of tomato, used as a garnish, should have been tossed. A stale hard roll, once soft, jumped in protest when Jones tried to cut it in half. Jones's hands were big, strong. The cheap plastic knife snapped in half and fell on the floor between us. The cubicle space was tight. The food was less than mediocre. Jones laughed at the absurdities. I laughed with him.

In that microsecond, when both us were laughing, the truth hit me—bam!

When this great man, great of size and career stature, approached the little woman in front of him, it was with a deep-founded fear.

He was stressed. He was tired. He was hungry. This is the precise formula that leads to stuttering. He didn't want to stutter in front of me, in our interview. He didn't know that even if he had stuttered, I would not have mentioned it.

Mrs. John Glenn, Annie, as she was known, was the wife of the astronaut turned Senator. Before I met Annie, the Senator beckoned me into his Washington office, closed the door and asked a favor. Please do not quote Annie verbatim if she stutters. I assured him I was, am, a legitimate journalist who would not quote a stutterer stuttering.

Annie, a lovely woman, had barricaded herself in a little room adjacent to the Senator's office. She was scared, wouldn't come out until the Senator went in, gave her a bear hug, and assured her I was "all right." Mrs. Glenn was a better interview than she thought she was. I never mentioned her stutters, and stutter she did. I did not broach the subject of stuttering. Annie wanted to talk only of John.

Jones, though, was up-front about his stuttering. Brought it right out in the open. I admired and respected him for the glow of the forthrightness that syncopated the interview.

"I was a stutterer. I've learned how to function in spite of it. But once a stutterer, always a stutterer. I'm a stutterer for life. I stutter under stress. When I'm not under stress, I choose words I know I can say."

Jones conquered his flaw, became the actor's actor, did a Robert Browning turnaround:

So take and use Thy work!
Amend what flaws may lurk.

I asked Jones how he'd mastered his voice, made it his superb instrument?

He said he'd become fascinated with the fact that, as an actor, his role was to relate his words to the listener's imagination, make the listener see pictures in the words he spoke or, better, feel the emotions concealed in the words.

"The job of acting involves opening yourself up. We use the author's words, but we also use everything that's in us. We present our voices and our bodies…. Actors use everything in them, especially the spirit."

One last question. I saved it for the end.

Every time I got anywhere near a "father" question, Jones concentrated on that terrible tuna salad, the rotting tomato. The interview, which he'd extended, was over. I took a last chance. If he said anything quotable about his father, wonderful. If he didn't, we still had a wonderful conversation.

Did you and your father ever reconcile? I said.

Jones cut me off like a gentleman. He told me I was a fine luncheon companion, thanks for coming and, with those workman boots, the poet marched off, leaving me alone with my notes, with my thoughts, with my admiration.

Later, I read in an NPR report out of Washington that Jones, an inspiring actor, went to New York City and found his father, still an aspiring actor.

Jones performed a difficult monologue of the impulsive young soldier, Hotspur, from Shakespeare's *Henry IV* just for his father.

He called that moment his "big audition." Using his magnificent voice, he delivered the tricky poetry of Shakespeare's play without a hitch.

There was no stuttering.

It was Daddy's turn to be silent.

Truman Capote

On loneliness at the top...

Stardom can offer airtight insulation from reality.
-Richard Corliss, Time Magazine, Oct. 30, 1995

Truman Capote, sloshed, was at home. This was not Breakfast at Tiffany's. We were in a Boston bar, the cocktail hour. Upscale bars were Capote's favorite domiciles, his places of worship, his beloved Mecca of spirits.

When he wobbled into view, the *maitre d'* pointed me out, and Capote ambled unsteadily to our cozy reserved table for two. It was obvious that the dwarfed, barely five-feet-two man with a squeaky, falsetto voice was intoxicated. He plopped-flopped opposite me. His elegant pinstripe Dunhill suit, perfectly pressed, had a stale bar smell that no dry cleaner could ever erase.

His slurred greeting was a mere mumble. He couldn't remember my name even when I told him. The only reality that registered on his foggy brain was the word "interview."

"Is that why we're together?" the scoundrel asked innocently.

I knew Capote couldn't see clearly. The bar lighting was dusky, lights low, and he was further blinded by Jackie-O oversized sunglasses with black lenses. I took no chances with an inebriated man wearing dark designer sunglasses in the shaded indoors.

"Yes, an interview," I said definitively, positively, conclusively.

On purpose, and flouting the stubborn mischief of a naughty child, he drowned out my "yes" with an overriding yell. "Waiter! Waiter!"

Instantly, a tuxedo-clad pretty boy, wearing curls and pink lipstick, materialized at his side. Capote asked for liquid sustenance. The waiter shoved a bar menu under his nose, stuck a pen in his swollen hand and Capote automatically scribbled a totally illegible autograph for the Lipstick Man.

Soon, too soon, I discovered that Capote's drink of preference was that remarkably magic potion, the straight-up vodka martini. He liked it served in a steady stream, one after the other, two or three gulps per drink. His capacity for the stuff appeared boundless. He'd already been served, and downed one martini. Another was way on the way. There was always another on the way.

Capote, then very rich and very famous, thanks to his brilliant *In Cold Blood* bestseller, owned a fancy, splendidly-equipped Jaguar executed in a streak of silver. He wasn't much good behind the wheel. Guess why.

We were facing each other across that small table in a richly brocaded hotel bar that mimicked the mysteriously drab elegance of a private, members-only London club. The place was more cocoon than saloon.

It also hinted of a certain waspish exclusivity. High-class Boston bars are like that. This one had a smoky, one-way glass wall that fronted a main thoroughfare. Passers-by couldn't see in. But bar patrons could see out. At that moment, no guest was interested in street goings-on.

The thrill was inside, seated at my table.

Not only was Capote wearing those pitch-black sunglasses, he hadn't bothered to remove his spotless, white felt gangsta fedora, rimmed in licorice grosgrain and cocked rakishly over one eye. Loneliness, and by god Capote oozed loneliness, made the man into an extreme extremist.

The flashy hat, the kind of fashion beacon you see paraded on a Rome Alta Moda runway, had alerted far too many bar patrons that they were actually in very close proximity to the great little Truman Capote. He was at the peak of his literary powers then and very recognizable. He was also a conspicuous showoff who reveled in his conspicuousness.

All eyes were riveted on him. Who wouldn't want to stare at this odd, famous drunk wearing a magnificent hat? And, because I was the other half of the interview, I was subject to the same stares. I was not, never will be, a performer pandering to a public audience. I am a newspaper journalist who talks privately, one-on-one, with legends.

We were onstage.

Politely, more politely than necessary, I asked him to remove his Jackie-O sunglasses. I wanted him (us) to fade into the scenery. I didn't mention removing the fedora. I thought it was asking for too much, too soon. I just wanted to see his eyes, bloodshot or not. I wanted to see the famous face, all of it, study the range of expressions, hang on his every word.

"No chance," he harrumphed about ditching the sunglasses. Why? asked I.

Blame my mother, he snarled.

When Capote's "mother" reference dropped out of the sky and into my lap, his frivolous expression suddenly turned sour. He droned on and on, incoherently, about his mother. Everyone was tuned in. Several times, he made the old-fashioned cross-your-heart-and-hope-to-die gesture. He wanted the bar guests to believe he was speaking the truth, convoluted as it was. I couldn't help but notice his hands. Small. Silky. A woman's hands.

I already knew all about his mother, so I'll fill you in more coherently than Capote spoke to the bar people. She married at fifteen. Produced a son. Got divorced. Shoved her cranky, wailing kid into the unwilling arms of two maiden aunts who knew nothing about raising babies. Nor were they interested in learning.

The saga mesmerized the bar patrons when Capote went several emotional steps further. He said that he never got any cooing, kissing, cuddling. All he ever saw scrolled across the faces of those dour aunts was condescension. He called the aunts "cold blooded" caretakers. They didn't care about taking care of him.

Capote didn't say all this in one fell swoop, like I'm telling you. He spoke in bits and pieces, snippets of this and that, jigsaw-puzzle language.

That day, the bar patrons witnessed what they never dreamed possible: A reality television show starring Truman Capote, in the flesh, drunk, telling his troubles out loud. He seemed to address them, not me. Practically everything he said was punctuated with a trill of silly tee-hees, which made the show more interesting. He'd arrived in a state of oblivion. He sank deeper into oblivion with each oncoming drink. Yet, like some drunks, Capote became more lucid at the peak of his drinking. For a moment, while riding high, he answered some of my questions poignantly.

Those dark glasses, the ones I'd asked him to remove, were a very important item in his life. He told me that sunglasses were how he liberated himself from his aunts' dirty looks and cold shoulders.

"Somehow, they made me feel apart but not necessarily attractive. It took courage for me not to give in to all the bullying. When I was about thirteen, I just went out and bought myself a pair of dark glasses to hide behind. I suppose it was a defense thing."

Capote never took them off except to sleep.

That's how he kept his aunts at bay. That's how he was keeping me at bay. Dark sunglasses and strange hats were his crutch. They hid half his face. Even when Capote gave his much-hyped Black and White Ball at New York City's Plaza Hotel, he wore a Lone Ranger half-mask. He was always more comfortable with his eyes concealed rather than revealed. There's an old Yiddish saying that eyes are the mirror of the soul.

But I'm in trouble here.

The "Tiny Terror," as he was widely known, was in command of the bar audience. He, an exquisite writer, knew that a journalist has to be in command of the interview, orchestrate it, lead it, steer it, get it on track. Capote was not so drunk that he didn't sense my distress. It amused him.

He turned his dark shades on me and, for no reason, quipped: Tee Hee!

Then he pulled the unconscionable. He pretended that I was

a broadcast journalist, and that, somehow, he never explained how, there were hidden cameras out there, somewhere around the bar. He said my notebook was really a microphone disguised. I handed him my notebook and pen. Inspect them, I said. He shoved them back. Slid them across the table. Didn't look at them.

Capote squeaked, loud enough to be heard by the bar people and an assortment of waiters who'd assembled to gape and eavesdrop, that he liked to go to "big-shot parties" — meaning that hosts had to be famous enough to draw a gaggle of paparazzi to their front doors. Capote, who loved to drop famous names, had recently attended a lavish, black-tie party at Gloria Vanderbilt Cooper's place in New York City.

"When the sidewalk reporters saw me get out of my car, they cheered and clapped and said I was the prettiest of all. When I got upstairs, they all blushed and twittered. Someone commented he always knew I'd blow my lid."

Tee hee…tee hee!

The paparazzi furor was caused by Capote's deliberate fashion *faux pas*. He'd topped classic tuxedo pants with an inexpensive Bill Blass sweater. It was a time when fashion-conscious people took serious fashion seriously. He was also a conspicuous showoff, a rebel, who reveled in his conspicuousness. This trait made him noticeable.

I wanted to ask Capote, an alcoholic, why his enormous success, his fame, didn't give him a measure of contentment. Instead, I asked Capote what his success meant to him. He lowered his voice. He spoke to me.

"Success doesn't give me euphoria. If anything, I get a mild case of post coital sadness. And when I have suffered violent attacks from enemies, I know it's all based on sheer envy – so I dismiss it. The only thing that really makes me angry is a vicious double-cross. But even that blows over in a half hour or so."

He probably meant a half hour or so of vodka martinis.

We'd been together about thirty minutes when everything changed for the worse. Capote turned up the volume and broadcast his sexual proclivity to the world-at-large – the bar people. Even drunk, he knew that he'd lost his initial audience, that more people had crowded in and paid him no heed. The curmudgeon, the rabble rouser, the rascal resorted to shock, very loud too.

"I-am-homosexual!" he yelled.

Well, who didn't know that?

Still, you could hear a pin drop, the bar got so hushed.

Quietly, as quietly as possible, I told Capote that his homosexuality had no bearing on the interview or on his talent. His shades were glued to my face. Instinctively, I knew there was more of this exhibitionist behavior to come. He whispered across the table that he didn't want to be known as a "fag."

I felt sorry for Capote.

The gossip then was that Princess Lee Radziwill, his friend and Jackie Onassis's sister, had referred to Capote as a fag. It got back to him. It hurt him. Now, getting more and more drunk, he used the word the princess had allegedly used. Capote had mentored the princess, who wanted to be an actress. He'd championed her ambitions. When she got disastrous reviews, when the critics killed her, he remained loyal. And then the "fag" talk.

But that day, drunk, Capote still spoke well of her.

"If she wasn't Jackie's sister, things would have gone better when she played in *Laura*. The critics would have said that she photographed well and acted adequately. But a lot of people transferred their resentment about the Kennedys to Lee."

I knew Capote was once in a serious car crash and, after extensive surgery, he fell into a deep depression, deeper than the one he was in then, when we met. His surgeon coaxed him into psychotherapy. He didn't like psychotherapy at all.

I asked him if psychotherapy and being in-interview had, ahem, commonalities?

"I guess I'm too headstrong. I always feel that I'm three or four jumps ahead of people. The psychiatrist was one of the best. But I knew intuitively what he was going to say. I refused to spend $75 an hour for predictable prophecy."

Capote suddenly asked where the television cameras were. Oh, not that again. I'm not a broadcast journalist, I tell him for the umpteenth time. He insisted there were cameras around, that I was "fooling" him.

By then, he was so far under the influence that he was beginning to babble.

"I feel very apart," he groaned. Then, incongruously: "The human existence is in a continuous state of crisis."

It was no secret that Capote had taken refuge in drugs other than alcohol.

"You are intensely happy for a moment. But while you're still happy, you can see that happiness has a shadow to it. Joy doesn't exist on its own. It's like orgasm. For a split second, you are in a state of physical joy, and that puts you out of control of yourself. Then there's that post coital sadness."

That was the second time he'd used the term "post coital."

The waiter, Mr. Lipstick, plunked down still another drink, maybe Capote's sixth.

Capote had told me lots, in a discombobulated way. I hadn't asked, but he volunteered that his friend Tennessee Williams, the eminent playwright, once queried him as to why he'd given up analysis.

"I told him that the doctor was beginning to interfere with my personal and private life."

And a few seconds later, he told me that courage is getting up in the morning (tee hee!), that hangovers aren't fun (tee hee!).

"Courage is sometimes a simple matter of live or die. But it takes a day or so to get my feet on the ground. So I just sit around and read 'til I feel like myself again."

I told Truman Capote that he was looking at a frustrated woman, that in no way could this be construed to be a civilized interview.

He retorted that I was looking at a man with a sad Alabama

childhood, a man who had a closet-rich apartment in the Big Apple's United Nations Plaza. He began to sound like his own bragging real estate agent. It was filled with antiques. It had a view of the East River. He had plenty of space to store his hats. He had hundreds of them. One hat was prized above all others, even more than the fedora still facing me.

"It's the Stetson the townspeople of Holcomb, Kansas, gave me after I researched *In Cold Blood*." I got really friendly with the whole town. The huntsmen contributed their wild pheasant feathers, and that's what decorates the crown."

Capote was now seven sheets to the winds. Seven or more drinks. He said whatever crossed his mind. I decided that I'd mention a famous name, someone he knew, and see what happened. This was my last-ditch effort. Tee hee was on his way to passing out.

Jacqueline Kennedy Onassis....

"She's a luxurious person. When she wants to turn on the charm, it flows like syrup in Vermont."

Christian Dior, the great Paris couturier....

"That man was a charming, well read, too-fat, pink imp who ordered a brioche as big as a cabbage and stuffed it with a half pound of butter."

Aristotle Onassis (I made no mention of the famous yacht)....

"It's a comfortable ship, but ugly. It's extremely opulent. Very badly done. It's really too much like an expensive suit in a not-precisely first class hotel."

Marilyn Monroe....

"She was living secretly with a man in a beach house near Los Angeles. He wasn't someone she married. One day, she couldn't resist going through his locked desk, where he kept a diary. The man didn't love her at all. He was making notes, which eventually would end up in a book about her lovemaking ability."

Balenciaga, the Paris couturier....

"He was a recluse who always dressed in black. I met him once at a Guinness party, and he looked like he belonged to the

Vatican. He presented a religious image, but I could not con-
fess to him."

Capote, exhausted, couldn't continue. He was slurring his
words, elongating them, mispronouncing them. There were
blank spaces between the words, like his brain was in fade-out.
His chin dropped involuntarily below the collar of his shirt and
stayed there. I saw the top of that damn fancy fedora, not
Capote's crumpled face. He mumbled something about want-
ing to leave now. Get a taxi.

The bar manager, a tall, burly man in a tuxedo punctuated
with a miniature orchid boutonniere, saw what was happening.
He came to Capote's rescue. He hoisted the drunk to his feet,
grabbed one arm. I grabbed the other. Together we leveraged
Capote toward the entrance to the hotel, toward a taxi stand.

Capote was gone. Something bad could happen to him. A
mugger. An accident. It turned out that Capote had someone
out there watching over him. A limo chauffeur, probably his
bodyguard in uniform, cap and all, dashed toward Capote. He
grabbed the fedora in his fist, took off Capote's dark glasses
and tossed both accessories on the front seat as if they were
junk.

And, as if he were manipulating a rag doll, he folded Capote
into a ball and plopped him on the back seat. Capote must have
thought he was in bed. He was curled into the fetal position,
fast asleep in the slinky black memo.

I would have liked to pursue another interview with Capote,
a more sober one. But Capote died before that happened, in
1984.

Then, by that indefinable element we call chance, I met
Dominick Dunne. Dunne had gone to Capote's funeral. I didn't
know that. Dunne and Capote were good friends. I didn't know
that either.

Dominick Dunne projected the air of a man who belonged to
the privileged class. What was not necessarily his by birth he
assumed through his enormous success as a Hollywood pro-

ducer and bestselling author. He's Irish Catholic, a fighter, a great dresser, and his shock of white hair has always been styled by a talented scissorshand. He has enemies. He's afraid of nothing and nobody. So everybody, even those who despise him or fear him, don't get too close. Those in his inner circle, a few true-blue friends, know that his bark has no bite.

Dunne and I were having a lovely lunch at Boston's Four Seasons Hotel. He spoke of his daughter, Dominique, his namesake, an attractive 21 year-old actress, who had been strangled by her boyfriend, a Hollywood chef, about three days away from being released from prison.

He damned the murderer without raising his voice, the same even-toned voice he'd used to order ice cream with chocolate sauce for our dessert.

I am, by nature, an emotional creature. I couldn't imagine how Dunne could keep his cool while talking about his offspring's violent murder. He smiled — you know Dunne's withering smile, tinged with slight sarcasm — the one he now uses on Court TV – and asked if I'd remembered a specific scene in one of his novels, the one where the mother of a murdered son takes a riding crop and thrashes violently at her pillow, reducing it to shreds.

"I did that myself, in my bedroom," Dunne said, not batting an eyelash. "It was as if I was beating my child's murderer."

Dunne is a wonderful *Vanity Fair* columnist. He had been an A-list movie producer (*Panic in Needle Park*, *The Boys in the Band*, *Ash Wednesday*) but staged his own get-away when, much to his chagrin, he began to hate Hollywood and its inbred phoniness.

He rented a decrepit, one-room cabin in the wilds of Oregon's Cascade Mountains, in the middle of nowhere. He went from a Hollywood mansion to a humble cottage where the linoleum was worn, the one battered chair was Naugahyde®, and the old wood table wiggled because the legs weren't even. It was there, alone in the wilderness, that he thought things out. He discovered that he no longer wanted to fraternize with the too-rich and too-famous.

Dunne wanted to move through life at an ordinary pace, mixing with ordinary people, doing ordinary things.

"During this time, I got a fantastic letter from Truman Capote," he said casually – almost as an afterthought.

Truman Capote! What about Truman Capote?

I never mentioned to Dominick Dunne that I'd "interviewed" Capote while he was drunk. And all of a sudden, Dunne brought up Truman Capote. Was this an eerie message from the grave? I don't know. All I know is that Dominick Dunne told me everything I'd wished Capote would have told me about himself.

"He (Capote) had heard from someone that I just dropped out of my life. It was a letter of admiration, encouragement. One sentence still stands out in my memory. 'Remember this: That is not where you belong (in Oregon), and when you get out of it what you went there to get, you've got to come back. Remember that.'

"When Truman died, I went to his memorial service. I listened to his friends talk about him. I listened to them read from his work. And I was overcome with a thought that hit me like a thunderbolt. When Truman wrote to me, it was exactly what he wished for himself. It's ludicrous that he's dead. If only he had separated himself from the 'ladies.' An author is still a journalist, a reporter. A reporter cannot become a part of whatever it is he or she covers. A barrier must remain between you and 'it.' How can you really listen to the voices you hear if your own voice is blurred with theirs?

"Truman became too involved in the lives of his subjects. He became a pet of society rather than an observer. He told the 'secrets' his 'ladies' told him. And then the 'ladies' banished him from their world. This caused him tremendous pain. He was the insider who became the outsider."

Ralph Lauren

On dressing for power...

**If there is a cornerstone to emotional
intelligence on which most other
emotional skills depend, it is a sense
of self-awareness, of being smart about
what we feel"**
-Nancy Gibbs, Time *Magazine, Oct. 2, 1995*

An item in *Parade*, the great Sunday newspaper supplement, caught my eye. A reader, Bryan Macuba from Ridgefield, Connecticut, the old New England town where I was born, was curious about Ralph Lauren's assumed aristocratic lineage. The world-famous designer's logo-of-choice, Polo, opened up a Pandora's box of the fashion designer's social/familial credentials.

"My wife says designer Ralph Lauren's real name is Lawrence. I say Lauren is his real name, and he's a polo star. Who's right?" Macuba asked (Aug. 12, 2001).

"Neither of you," *Parade* responded with pithy finesse. "The 61 year old Bronx-born designer changed his name from Lifschitz to Lauren while in high school, thinking it would look better on the clothing he hoped to make. His siblings followed suit. The closest he comes to a polo field is the logo on his merchandise."

There was, of course, no mention of Lauren's current net worth (billions?).

There were no references to his real estate holdings, which reportedly included a Fifth Avenue duplex overlooking Central Park, a twenty-nine acre Jamaica hideaway set in a tropical jungle with its own swimming pool hugging the sea, and a rambling, 6,000 acre Colorado ranch.

Later, some of the automotive jewels from his vast collection of rare classic cars would be displayed for public viewing, with ticketed prices and long lines, in a unique showroom: Boston's world-esteemed Museum of Fine Arts (2005). What mesmerized the anxious crowds was a different kind of fine art — sleek, spotless car stars from another era, another lifestyle:

Bugatti, Mercedes-Benz, Jaguar, Ferrari, *et-cet-er-a*.
Then there were, still are, his everyday perks. The snazzy private plane. His custom-made Porsche with every possible luxury, the one he takes for a spin when limos become tiresome and boring.

When Ralph Lauren stares out of his colorful cowboy ads – usually in two-page spreads – he looks like an old fashioned, gray-haired movie star, slick and sophisticated. The man's open road always seems unobstructed, smooth as silk, lucky. At least that's what the ads, and the satisfied expression in his eyes, suggests.

His starry life wasn't always starry.

When he was a kid, he yearned to be a professional basketball player. He's surprisingly short. Those eye-catching ads usually are shot from the thigh up. Lauren is a little guy. His smallness quashed the basketball dream.

He didn't start at the top of his fashion game. He launched his career insignificantly, as a tie salesman. That business failed. Without a steady cash flow, he was nearly broke. If anyone knows what "down and out" feels like, it's Ralph Lauren.

But one thing has always saved Lauren, salvaged his best dreams, put him way over the top. He convinced people that his brand of clothes – seasonless, classy classics – was what modern fashion is really about. It was at a time when the world's fashion leaders convinced consumers to throw everything out every six months – and start anew. It was a time of conspicuous consumption, when the world believed that couturiers were gods, before feminists labeled them dictators.

How did he do it? How did Ralph Lauren buck the whole powerful fashion-world system and become a household word around-the-world, respected and revered?

That's what this inquiring mind wanted to know.

A terrible blizzard was in fast progress. The weather outside was frightful. So was Lauren's health. I was in Ralph Lauren's

New York office, more functional than fancy. The man, shivering, was in the throes of a bad cold. His voice was a rasp. He was sneezing. When he coughed, it was to the tell-tale sound of mucus rattling deep. He needed a prescription cold medicine laced with codeine.

It was freezing in his office. The thermostat was turned down way too low. I'd kept my coat on. Lauren explained, his voice grating from a sore throat, that the problem was the heating system in the damn building.

Lousy!

The man wasn't dressed properly for winter weather indoors. He'd mixed a pair of old jeans with a badly wrinkled, blue denim shirt that looked as if he'd grabbed it straight out of the dryer. His shoes were old Indian moccasins. No socks. And maybe he was coming down with pneumonia.

Jeez.

In his office, just another workplace, stood a metal rack on wheels. It was hung with a charming array of eight-ply cashmere men's sweaters. The colors were lush. Grab one of them! The red one looks good! Warm yourself up!

That's what I suggested to the sick guy.

Ralph Lauren is the kind of designer who, on occasion, demonstrates his philosophy before he puts words to it. He answered in precise body language.

The man leapt from his old-fashioned swivel chair, the kind you spot as a good buy in garage sales in the countryside. He sprinted past the rack of gorgeous cashmeres and grabbed an antique Santa Fe afghan draped haphazardly on a nearby leather couch that had seen better days. In one swift Houdini move, whoosh, he wound it around himself tightly.

I was looking at a papoose.

Already I knew three things about Ralph Lauren: His immune system was totally out of whack. He wasn't exactly generous with his own cashmeres. And he wanted to see if the woman journalist, the one in love with words, was savvy enough to get his point via the power of suggestion

Lauren knew, intuitively, that I was aware that he, a fashion impresario, was playing the part of a native American for an awfully good reason. The cowboys and indians theme was then the subject of his advertising campaign, reportedly in the $10.5 million range. He showed me, by example, that his fashion theory is that some things never go out of style. Even when they're old, they become "classics."

I had to hand it to the man and his creative way with my interview. Afghans, like the one he wrapped himself in, are classics from another generation – grandma's. Moccasins are classics. I have a current Vermont Country Store catalog featuring authentic Indian moccasins touted as the ultimate in tootsie comfort. To label old jeans and mangled denim shirts mere classics would be a travesty. Denim is in everyone's wardrobe today – even Iraqi civilians caught in a terrible war. I see jeans every day in the news part of the newspaper, the one with those terrible photos of bloodied victims of war, wounded men on stretchers, writhing in pain, being rushed to primitive places called hospitals. They're wearing jeans. And, in the United States, on casual Fridays, jeans are *de rigueur*.

But then, on that snowy day, what Lauren was showing me was that planned obsolescence, the mainstay of the fashion industry, didn't cut it anymore. The cashmeres on that rack were v-neck slip-ons, executed in the best cashmere, a current mainstay at Harrods – or any fine men's boutique on London's Saville Row. The style of Ralph Lauren's clothes was made to last forever.

So I asked the papoose what it felt like to be a maverick, a man who dared to commit fashion heresy, declare war on the seasonal changes of everyone's wardrobe.

"I'm not in the business of change. I'm anti-fashion," the papoose said. "I've never really liked what's 'in.' I like things that have a sense of tradition. When something lasts, it suggests quality and integrity. It's something to cherish rather than discard. I'm thrilled when I see people wearing my ten-year old jackets."

When Lauren talked real clothes for real people at his staff meetings, people he trusted balked. Loyalty flew out the window. He'd raved about starting a new movement in fashion, a new wave. His reasoning was, is, that no person — man or woman – has the time, energy, dollars or closet space to change fashions every few months on the whim of some designer who's creating strange clothes in an ivory tower.

Nobody loves a pioneer. Who wants to back someone who's rocking the boat? There's too much risk involved. Close colleagues laughed in Lauren's face or behind his back. Some of his buddies, his so-called pals, jumped ship, quit to join forces with fashion houses that, indeed, made seasonal changes. Some of his friends were direct. They told him he was shooting himself in the foot. They warned he was committing career suicide.

"You have to believe in yourself even when they close the door," the papoose told me when I asked about what it felt like to be abandoned by people who'd been on his team.

There's an innate, lingering sorrow connected with people who unpledge their allegiance to you. Lauren, being Lauren, took a chance on himself. He went ahead, more or less on his own, and presented a collection of classic fashions, variations of which have always been around.

"American clothes," he called them. "The American look," he commented emphatically to anyone who'd listen.

Sales plummeted.

The business collapsed.

People like Ralph Lauren, who catapult themselves to the top, can look back at their failures, refer to them as milestones that marked their way to the top. I said exactly that to Lauren that day. Ordinary people can get mired in their losses. Some never find a way out. Determination and hard work doesn't always mean you're going to hit your mark.

The papoose's voice was rough around the edges because of the cold. He had a runny nose, constant, and he was fumbling for tissues. He coughed too much. But the phrasing of his answer was perfect. He spoke slowly, in strong, stand-alone sentences. He enunciated every word. He wanted me to "get it."

"I've never joined the fashion club. By that I mean I never did what everybody else was doing."

Achoo!

"And I didn't get the acceptance I thought I deserved. I'd failed. But failure is just a passage. You go down. You get up."

Achoo!

"I went from being a genius to a non-genius. You cry inside when this happens. You swallow it. But you go on. You have to believe you're special, that what you do is special.

"Even without praise, you've got to persevere, believe you're going to make it. I didn't have a support system. The cash flow was tight. I felt squeezed."

Achoo!

"I wasn't bankrupt. But it was getting dark. I shivered. People I trusted in the company left me. That's painful. You swallow it, but you go on.

"You want a good report card, positive recognition. You have to believe that you're special, that what you do is special.

"Even without praise, you've got to persevere."

Achoo!

Lauren was genuinely surprised when I told him this wasn't the whole answer. He was tired and felt awful, but I wanted more: Tell me how you persevered, how you went on, how you survived. It wasn't just your attitude. It was your attitude and something else.

That's when Lauren told me about the "something else," his primitive method of presenting himself to the world, dressing as if he was a powerful designer even when he wasn't.

The man is dancing in the dark, alone, and where's the power in that? At first I thought: The man is putting me on.

The more Lauren explained his psychology, the clearer his philosophy became. I had to acknowledge that, indeed, little things, like dressing distinctively, can mean a lot. How others perceive you, how you project your self-image, can be a kind of passport from a dark place to a new place. Clothes can be a mood changer, a light that you switch on yourself, like a self-oriented spotlight.

Lauren spoke to me about what we've put a name to now: emotional intelligence. This was the gist of his "something else."

Regardless of weather or season, he wore a crisp white suit, always in mint condition, with the best, the freshest, the most chic accessories he could muster. The loser presented himself as a winner. White is bright. It's an alive color. It represents a clean slate. Sometimes, when you fool others by dressing differently and with authority, you fool yourself. Your inner being starts to hum.

"My mother used to call dressing up basic 'first aid' when you're down in the dumps.

"On one rainy day, I was getting dressed to go to the office. I hated to go to the office in those days. But I wanted to show people that I still had my head up, despite it all.

"It was a very symbolic gesture, but I reached for a white suit that day. It was raining outside of me and inside of me. But the white suggested sunshine. You wear black to a funeral. You wear white to a party.

"I said to myself: I'll reach for something white, something sunny and bright. I can't go around fumbling in the dark. I've got to get in there and fight.

"From that day forward, things got better. I think it's how you perceive things. How you take the worst things and make them better."

The papoose, a diminutive Bronx guy born with the name Lifschitz, seemed ordinary on the outside. Inwardly, he was a tiger. When he failed – and he's the first to tell you his first venture/adventure into classics-as-fashion failed – he strutted around the fashion world in a nice white suit, ignoring his detractors. He created an image of being in command, of sureness. His doubters weren't exactly swayed. But they doubted less. And he got new backers.

I, a cynic, shot him my usual pessimism.

Hey, Ralph Lauren, I know you're talking symbolically, that the white suit represented a change of attitude, a change of outlook, a change in mood. It was a sign that suggested you could access your own strengths. Okay, the white suit worked like magic for you. It was impressive. It became your signature when your world turned dark. Other people, wearing white suits in similar situations, might not get such great results. So what's the difference between you and them?

"I'm talking about believing in your own rightness, your own correctness. That's what you communicate and that's what people react to.

"I trust my gut feelings about everything. I worry about health, deadlines, pressures. But instinct is something we all have. It's a voice that comes from somewhere in your stomach. It tells you if you're right or wrong.

"But sometimes you rationalize that voice away. You've got to trust your own hunches. Success is feeling good about yourself.

"I used to think fame was magic. I love magic and movie stars because they always seem to be walking on clouds.

"What I design is what I am. I'm not apart from what I do."

When the always white-suited Ralph Lauren started assembling a new staff, he made independent choices. When colleagues told him he was making the wrong choices, he didn't listen.

"I picked the president of my company against the advice of experts. He's a low-key guy, doesn't come on like dynamite. He's got the kind of personality that grows on you. He's not a one-shot type, someone who immediately convinces you he's going to take over the world. I had interviewed other worldly men who came in and made witty wisecracks. I went with my gut feelings of feeling good about him."

Ralph Lauren's white suit was emblematic of a new beginning.

Years later, after one of Ralph Lauren's spectacular New York fashion openings, his secretary tracked me down amidst the maddening media crowd and said that her boss would like to take me to lunch. He'd picked a date, a few days away. I thought he wanted to talk about this new collection, tell me more about what I'd seen.

By then, Polo/Ralph Lauren products had passed the $3.1 billion volume mark and were climbing higher and higher. The man didn't need to ride into battle on a cavalry horse. He had his white suit. That, and a lot of confidence.

It was a grand summer day. June.

Ralph Lauren and I were sauntering along Madison Avenue, New York City, checking out the boutiques. We'd just had a fabulous lunch on the sidewalk of a French bistro, sitting under a huge awning, not far from the historic Rhinelander Mansion, which would become his magnificent flagship store.

We'd chatted briefly about his new collection over lunch. Now we were entranced by the glorious weather. The gentle sunshine, the cloudless blue sky, the parade of people gliding by, "the people of summer," Lauren called them. We were even amused by the autograph hounds who thought nothing of barging into our conversation with scraps of paper and a pencil thrust under the star's nose.

When he'd dismissed his driver, Lauren said he wanted to walk with me.

Lauren loves flowers as much as I do. We especially gloated over the supremely talented florists who set their spotless glass windows ablaze with great vases of exotic flowers in intoxicating color combinations.

We peered inside old antique shops. Candy stores stocked with *bon bons* and, oh yes, elaborate chocolate trays. We looked at Persian rug boutiques. There were faux jewelry emporiums

— the most amusing being the one owned by Zsa Zsa Gabor's mother who, it was rumored, had more or less copied the great jewelry of Hungarian royalty from a library book. These days, Joan Rivers probably uses a similar tactic to sell her fake jewelry on QVC, the shopping network.

Then Lauren dropped a bomb.

I remember how, for no apparent reason, we'd stopped near the side entrance of The Pierre Hotel. He said something complimentary about our first big interview – the papoose one – and admitted that he was surprised at how well I'd understood his theories. He said he wanted to tell me about the art of recovery.

Those were his words: "the art of recovery."

I thought he was talking about the white suit, the role it played in rejuvenating his fallen empire.

That wasn't it at all.

He shocked me with his next words: "I've always appreciated life. After my surgery, that philosophy crystallized. I am more aware of drifting away."

People in the fashion industry twittered that Lauren had undergone serious surgery, but, to my knowledge, he'd never spoken specifically about it. Who wants to give hospitals, and all they imply, a second thought on a beautiful summer day? I, ever the journalist, asked: What kind of surgery?

"I had a brain tumor."

What?

"That's the most frightening thing that ever happened to me. At the same time I was on the cover of *Time*, a doctor was telling me: 'You have a tumor on your brain.'

"These were conflicting, seesaw images. Would anyone have traded places with me? I don't think so. Nobody would care about a magazine cover if it also meant having a brain tumor.

"It was a lonely time for me. I saw people rushing about with glum faces. I thought they were wasting time being unhappy. That gave me perspective. I began to see things differently, and I began to see myself differently. I saw everything differently.

"I'm making my time work. I like to make connections with people. Connections have to be based in reality or else they disappear. I think people should build and add to what they already have. I keep old friends and cultivate new ones.

"I love greatness. There's a purity to greatness. People who are really great don't think they're great. They do the best they can do. And they never think they've done all they can do."

That day, Ralph Lauren made me feel like a trusted professional friend, someone to whom he could speak confidences. I asked him if what he'd just told me, his specific comments, then generally unknown to the media, were on the record.

He said "yes."

I hugged him, in sincere thanks, spur of the moment, for his generosity of quotes. This was an unexpected gift of news to my newspaper and me. I'd taken down every word, using my briefcase as an impromptu lean-on, hoping the scoop was for headlines.

The man wasn't wearing a white suit. He sported a gray, three-piece vested suit. But to me, standing there in the sunshine on the sidewalks of New York, he was the papoose who'd metamorphosed into a knight on a white charger.

Norman Vincent Peale

On real guardian angels...

**We are all identical, scared and insecure
human beings, every last one of us."**
-Terri Williams, author
Boston Herald, *Nov. 14, 1994*

When I came home from work, spouting frustrations, she was my sounding board. When I told her about this or that crushing defeat I'd had at my newspaper, she'd dangle her guardian angel theory in my face. I didn't say what I really thought: *bah humbug.*

Mom, Anna was her name, listened to me. But I didn't listen to her, especially when she assured me that guardian angels hovered everywhere – even in the harsh jungle of journalism.

Anna was the woman who put all my hopeless situations into perspective and, through her unfathomable faith, propped me up until I found myself operating in the realm of hope again. It took me a million years to put the words "guardian angel" after her name. But, for a million years, she was exactly that.

Now she was dead. Cancer had eaten her alive.

I was there, in our pew at Trinity Church, Boston, alone, in the exact spot we'd sat together for years, every Sunday, before we headed for a little brunch somewhere. She taught me how to celebrate life. Now she was frozen dead, like a statue, stuck in that box they call a casket, gone forever.

The funeral service was the one she'd written herself, long before cancer shattered our life. On her deathbed, she made me promise again and again ("...yes, dear Mom, I promise!") to execute the details, the specifics, of her funeral and interment exactly. Don't pay attention to the scorch of interference from clergy or her other children, she'd warned. Now, remembering, I see that she'd expected me to be her guardian angel.

Music was one of her favorite languages.

The last words I heard, as I followed her box down the mile-long church aisle, was the essence of a goodbye promise. "God Be With You Till We Meet Again," a male voice sang out. His voice caressed the rafters. The words entered my ears, but they never reached my heart.

Meet again? Nonsense! How could Anna think her funeral was not The End for her and, thus, for me? We would not be meeting again. Heaven, that endless desert up there, is too vast, too mysterious, to be a believable rendezvous of the future. Once, before she died, her tongue stumbled over the word "orphan."

"You'll have to stand alone," she muttered, "but a guardian angel will find you, orphan girl."

I thought she'd been needled with too much morphine.

Anna accepted the x-factors of life. Not silly Ouija board stuff or History Channel specials about hauntings and witches and fortune tellers. Anna knew about the essence of angels. She gambled that I'd figure out that we could communicate through other people, a third party, under surprise circumstances. She could always identify strangers of exceptional sensitivity — people who did the right thing, said the right words, acted the right way at the right time.

She recognized the Samaritans who were equipped with extraordinary radar, a capacity to operate on a very high frequency. Those were the wings on which she thought guardian angels flew.

Immediately after her burial in Mount Auburn Cemetery, Cambridge, I went directly from her grave to my newspaper cubicle. It was the only hiding place I knew. As I sat there, my coat still on, watching my newspaper operate as usual, I made an ironclad decision. Journalism would be my refuge, my crutch, my everything.

It didn't work.

I was always looking for earthly glimpses of Anna, standing at the big picture window that dominated our small living room, waving hello as I pulled into the driveway after a long workday. I thought I saw her shadow dashing around corners. I sipped tea in the small cafes we'd frequented, pretending she was a little late, that she'd show up any second and we'd share a scone and raspberry jam.

Illusions.

I mourned Anna for a long time. Too long. Held the grief inside like a heavy weight that bogged me down. I was in a prison of my own making. I worked until I was weary, weak and sleepy.

Sleep didn't stop the mourning. I always dreamed of Anna.

My editor beckoned me to his office. He was intrigued with a world-famous theologian, Dr. Norman Vincent Peale, whose primary pulpit was the Marble Collegiate Church, New York City. Standing room only.

People queued around the block to hear the preacher who didn't preach, but spoke off the cuff, in modern parables. The editor wanted me to interview The Pulpit Man, see if he was "for real."

It was being argued, then, that Dr. Peale, more than any other man of his time, made God believable to millions of unbelievers. It was Dr. Peale who'd coined the indelible phrase, "The Power of Positive Thinking," and turned his concept into an international best seller (1952). Peale made Jesus Christ a Superstar long before Andrew Lloyd Webber thought of it in rock opera form (1971).

Huge auditoriums, where his name lit the marquee, attracted audiences of 10,000 or more. The Pulpit Man always seemed to be talking about troubles — both the everyday kind and the ones that are life-numbing.

Who among us doesn't want to know why God can't control trouble?

Dr. Peale's office was drenched in red. Red carpeting. Red drapes. Furniture upholstered in red. It was the pure red of cardinals, both the birds and the ecclesiastics. Television stars lean on red to connote their power. That red inner sanctum vibrated with Peale power, the kind that envelopes you, puts you in a trance, suggests cheer.

I was not susceptible to cheer.

Dr. Peale was eighty three then, a robust, beardless Santa Claus type with a double chin and thick spectacles. When he walked in, portly, small stature, tall posture, with his red tie juxtaposed against a white shirt, he seemed to radiate energy. His suit was black, parson-like, severe, like those worn by Anglican clerics.

Holy-looking? No. Dashing? Yes.

I'd researched The Pulpit Man. My dossier was typed up like a lawyer's brief. I was all business. Impromptu questions rattled around in my brain. I knew I didn't look good. I hated my mirror reflection. My complexion was grayed. I was still recovering from "walking pneumonia." I'd worked while sick of body, sick of spirit, and pretended to be oozing strength.

I didn't fool The Pulpit Man.

Dr. Peale took one hard look at me and said something outrageous.

"You're carrying a burden."

I retorted, with anger that matched the red room, that he'd made an offensive assumption. I was there to interview him. Let's keep this professional. He ignored my emotionally-charged outburst, didn't move a muscle.

"Has somebody you loved just died?" he asked softly, benevolently.

I shot eye daggers at him, but they turned moist. My defense mechanism snapped into place.

Maybe the Pulpit Man had checked me out thoroughly, as thoroughly as I'd researched him. Maybe some interfering, nincompoop editor at the newspaper had given him TMI (too much information). If so, that would mean that my impersonal front was transparent.

"Did you lose your mother?" he asked gently.

Anna! He referenced Anna! I wanted to escape. But you can't run from sorrow. It follows you everywhere because it's inside you, and everywhere you go, it goes. I reached for my coat, ready to flee. I was unable to move.

"When did your mother die?"

Dr. Peale's voice seemed to come from a distance. Indistinctly, almost in spite of myself, I murmured something about Anna's funeral being yesterday. I knew it wasn't a recent yesterday. It was a long ago yesterday. I couldn't remember which yesterday. I'd completely lost my cool.

"How did your mother die?

When he used the word "mother" again, I wanted to scream. No sound came out. I wanted to dump the blasted interview, the career, get out of there. In truth, The Pulpit Man found the hole in my soul and addressed it. But his pointed questions cut like a serrated knife.

Dr. Peale was a people genius. He'd seen the stoop of my shoulders, heard my rage. That didn't stop him. He harked back on the mother-who-died subject like a puppy refusing let go of the bone.

"How are you coping with her death?" he ventured, moving closer, deeper into the root of my bad personal situation. I was aware that he sounded like a therapist, only nicer.

Suddenly I heard a voice, it couldn't be my voice, asking Dr. Peale if he was conducting some survey on death? Like, say, the impact of death on loved ones left behind? Am I going to be the subject of your next sermon? My voice was caustic.

Then, I blurted: Sorry, Dr. Peale. Sorry.

I was stuck between a rock and a hard place. This man had maneuvered me onto the threshold of some kind of spiritual release that started with my identifying the pain, giving it a name. I have no idea how he honed in on me so carefully, so expertly. He'd grabbed my territory, the interview, and made it his.

Was The Pulpit Man in collusion with Anna? How come he was asking me about her? I started to cry, couldn't help it. And on company time, too! Copious tears flowed. Sobs that would not be squelched made me gulp for air. This was what should have happened privately before the funeral, or after the funeral. Dr. Peale stood there, letting me rid myself of the old despair. He handed me tissue after tissue which, when drenched, he dropped in a wastebasket near his desk.

"Tell me what you're feeling now," he prodded ever so kindly. This was the question the priest who conducted my mother's funeral never asked. No one ever asked me that question. I said something like that.

When I'd finally calmed down, I said okay, let's do the interview. He'd taken off his glasses. And that's when I saw him wipe away his own tears, using tissues from the same box he'd accessed on my behalf.

The famous man had cried tears of sympathy for and with me.

"My mother died on a Saturday morning, and I had a speaking engagement the next day," Dr. Peale said to me, the red-eyed journalist scribbling her notes.

"I loved my mother dearly. I asked the Lord: Do I have what it takes to speak? I thought I heard my mother say: 'Don't moon around. Do your job.'

"The next day, I went to the train…and into the train came a friend of mine, a big, burly fellow, a colonel. We said 'hello.' He asked where I was going. I told him I was on my way to preach a sermon. He said he was going to a clambake.

"After awhile, the colonel said: 'What's the matter with you? You're not acting like yourself.' I told him my mother had just died. He didn't say a word. When we got to his stop, he didn't get off.

"'Why?' I asked him. He told me he'd decided not to go the clambake, that since it was a Sunday he felt he should come to church to listen to me preach. Well, after church, he took me to lunch and, after that, to the train.

"Before saying goodbye, he said: 'You've seen me through some tough ones. God sent me along to be with you today.' That's all he said. And he walked off.

"People are always asking me how to express love. Sometimes it's not what you say but what you do."

That's how the Pulpit Man, then at the apex of his enormous success, defined "guardian angel" his way, but it was linked to her way, Anna's concept of guardian angels as good people.

Dr. Peale folded his arms across his abundant chest, leaned back in his swivel chair set on rollers, pushed himself a foot or two farther away from me, the way photographers do to get long shots, and asked:

"Do you know what 'cold courage' means?"

I know. But I thought he probably knew much better. This is the only famous man I've ever interviewed who asked *me* questions, turned the interview into a psychological probe. And I let him get away with it. He mesmerized me. But I knew I was swimming in unknown waters.

I didn't answer his question about cold courage. So he asked it another way, a more personal way.

"Have you ever met anyone who exhibited cold courage?"

Yes.

"Tell me everything you know about that person."

I knew his tactic. He wanted to know if I understood the meaning of courage and if, by verbalizing it, I had some of the same stuff in me.

I've never allowed an interview to be focused on me, become so personal. I'd never cried in an interview either. The savvy Pulpit Man kept our talk generic. It never seemed he was talking about me. But he was.

And I told him about the "cold courage" of a man called Harold Russell.

Both his hands were hooks. When we met for an interview, he extended his right hook in a handshake. It was Russell's instant check of a woman's reaction to the cold touch of an ugly hook. I shook the hook as if it were skin and bones.

Surprised, the man didn't say "hello." He said: "Gee, thanks, lady!"

"How did he lose his hands?" Dr. Peale asked.

Russell was a twenty-three year-old demolition sergeant wearing all the right protective gear. At exactly 1:35 p.m. on June 6, 1944, at Camp McCall, near Durham, New York, he was showing his men how to attach a detonator to nitro-starch – an explosive that's like dynamite.

The explosive had been sitting in the field too long, heated up by the sun. In one terrifying instant, when Russell touched the cap to the detonator, it exploded and blew off both his hands.

In the hospital, in traction, temporarily blinded and in horrific pain, he told me he despised the surgeons who told him, don't-worry-buddy-you'll-be-outfitted-with-hooks.

Russell hollered back, "Son-of-a-bitch, can't you acknowledge that I have no hands?"

I was on the verge of apologizing for repeating Russell's vulgarity, but Dr. Peale just said: "Go on."

Someone had to feed Russell.

He couldn't go to the toilet on his own, not even to pee, and he certainly couldn't light or hold a cigarette. Russell told his doctors that he wanted to die. They put hooks where his hands used to be.

Then a Charlie MacDonegal, a successful real estate agent, a stranger who'd heard about Russell's accident, stopped by his hospital room. MacDonegal's hands had been blown off in battle.

He put his hooks up to Russell's hooks and said, "Hey, I'm going through life with no hands, and so can you!"

"Yes?" Dr. Peale prodded.

Russell started bawling. He cried like me, like I just did, and he told MacDonegal that you can't make love to a woman when you have hooks, and what was life without love? MacDonegal told Russell to assume what's now known as "attitude." If Russell acted as if the hooks didn't matter, others would react the same way.

Russell cried more, called himself a misfit.

MacDonegal responded by throwing a silver dollar in the air with one hook and catching it with the other. Try it, he challenged Russell. When Russell mastered this trick, MacDonegal convinced him it was a sign that nothing was impossible.

The Army was doing a documentary, *Diary of a Soldier.* MacDonegal made some calls, pulled strings. He thought that Russell, a soldier with two hooks where his hands ought to be, should be the narrator. Russell played to the camera like a natural-born actor.

Guess who saw the documentary?

"Who?" asked Dr. Peale, hanging on my every word.

William Wyler, the legendary Hollywood producer who made Bette Davis a superstar. Wyler telephoned Russell to ask if he'd test for the part of Homer Parrish, a handless sailor, in an upcoming movie, *Best Years of Our Lives.* Russell thought his drinking buddies were playing a practical joke. He slammed the phone in Wyler's ear.

"And?"

Wyler called right back, said, "Don't hang up! It's really me, Billy. I want you for that part."

That's how Russell, a man with hooks, played a man with hooks. He walked away with two unprecedented Oscars: for Best Supporting Actor and a second Honorary Academy Award for Courage. Russell also walked away from Hollywood, founded a consulting firm for the handicapped, married, became a widower and married again.

Now *you* tell *me* about cold courage, I said to The Pulpit Man.

"Today, on my desk, is a letter from a mother who told me about her son, her only child. She described him as a nice boy. He came home to his apartment and was set upon by three robbers. One brutally attacked and murdered him. Now, the mother writes, you tell me how I can deal with this? She is alone. A widow. She described her son as the idol of her life.

"When I read the letter, I was inwardly disturbed. And I wrote her a letter just now. I told her my heart went out to her in sympathy and understanding. For me to say I 'understood' was a little forced. But, in the name of God, I told her I loved her. Then I told her the world is full of trouble, that trouble comes unexpectedly.

"She'd raised the 'why' of it. 'Why' did this have to happen? It didn't make sense. I don't know why. But I told her that a good mother is the nearest thing to human perfection. She'd raised a boy who was a credit to her. Therefore she has a residue of courage and faith. I told her not to torture herself with the 'why.'

"The 'why' is imponderable."

Dr. Peale suddenly switched the interview back to Harold Russell.

"Do you remember anything else Russell said about 'cold courage?'"

Yes.

Russell had been shipped to Walter Reed Hospital, where he'd been sent for additional stomach surgery. They stuck him in the amputee ward. He was shocked to hear a false rumor-of-hope whispered from bed to bed.

Russian doctors had discovered a way to successfully reattach limbs. It was the big news of the day. The amputees told each other that their American counterparts, the surgeons, could pull the same feat. Russell said "the boys" debated who'd be first on the doctor's operating list.

It was Russell, with his hooks, who told his fellow amputees the truth. Their limbs, like his limbs, had been blown to smithereens. There were no limbs to reattach.

Dr. Peale embellished Russell's courage story with the kind of spoken elegance that had made him a famous preacher.

"You and I, all of us, have minds and spirits encased in what they call the physical body. You don't see the mind or the spirit. You only see the workings of the mind and the spirit. We dream, we think, we decide, we consider through that instrument called mind. I'm an old fashioned preacher who believes the soul is in the mind."

Why is God, whom, it is reported, actually answers prayers, so relentless about putting all kind of obstacles in the way of people? I asked him that.

"This is my idea of God," Dr. Peale said. "He wants to develop strong people. And you can't develop strength without roadblocks, difficulty, pain, fighting.

"Once I talked to Gene Tunney, the fighter, who had a straight up-and-down waistline, and mine was not. He said that the stomach muscles grow flabby and sag if you don't exercise.

"Tunney told me that exercise is the practice of resistance, that resistance is the strengthener, the tightener. You toughen your mind and your spirit when you meet difficulties. I don't like difficulties. But God doesn't want weak, flabby people. He wants people to stand up valiantly, to meet the resistance."

Dr. Peale's stories were all aimed at bringing a measure of comfort to me. No fancy theologian reasoning was offered. No Bible quotes. Just two people talking, nice and easy, as if this wasn't an interview at all. Without preaching, the world-famous Pulpit Man urged me to air the grief buried in the archives of my soul, unearth them, set them free and, thus, set myself free.

He gave me powerful quotes but, in the process, he elicited powerful quotes from me.

I don't remember seeing any crosses in Dr. Peale's red room. There were no candles. There were no fancy outward signs to connect him to any rich church. The Pulpit Man needed none of the luxuries associated with holy places.

Dr. Peale never told my editors that I'd cried.

I never told them either.

When I turned in my story, I asked my editor if anyone at the newspaper had talked to Dr. Peale about me in advance of our meeting? No. Had my editor mentioned my mother's death to him? No. No one had spoken to him.

No one, except...Anna? Could it really be?

This is how I learned what Anna knew all along, that guardian angels are efficient human beings who are there when you need them most. They can see what needs to be done, and they do it.

I never met or talked with Dr. Peale again.

When I read his obituary in 1993, I remembered what he told me about death and dying:

"Consider a baby in his mother's womb. He's got to be born, to die out of that place. If the baby could speak, he'd probably say: 'I'm warm here. I'm fed. I don't want to leave.' But he's told in nine months, he'll have to leave this place, be born into something else. When he is born, he is dying out of the womb, finding himself in loving arms with loving faces looking down at him."

Dying, he'd said, was like being born in reverse. Dr. Peale assured me that my mother, like his mother, like all good people who die, had fallen into the presence of a beautiful "Being."

When I grabbed my briefcase, he said something very personal, eerie almost. He told me that those who've disappeared from our lives have a way of leaving messages "here and there."

Stephen Hawking

On hope where there is none...

Hope is like a road in the country:
There was never a road, but when many
people walk on it, the road
comes into existence."
-Lin Yuang, dancer

I am looking into the icy eyes of a man buried alive.

He's stuck, glued, strapped into an automated wheel chair, a futuristic magic marvel, so technologically complicated that it looks like a prop from *Battlestar Galactica*.

His body is gnarled, twisted into a zigzag position, sitting crookedly, which is, for him, straight. Rivals, insanely jealous that this severely disabled man is currently the world's most famous living scientist, forgot that his ears still work.

They dubbed him "The Crip," as if he didn't know.

Dr. Stephen Hawking, considered the Einstein of our time, is saddled with Lou Gehrig's disease, incurable. What this means is that every day his body shuts down a little more, dies off. On the other hand, what do doctors really know? They handed him their grim reaper verdict when he was twenty-one: He had two, maybe three years left.

Hawking is sixty five years old as I tell you this. I've always thought it weird, ironic, that he was born on Jan. 8, 1942, 300 years to the day of Galileo's death.

His rich friends, he has many, gladly give him the use of their magic carpets, staffed private planes – one of which is how he landed in Boston, in my neighborhood, in my presence. He and his synthesizer speak at universities around the world. His annual income is said to be in the $2 million range.

Queen Elizabeth bestowed on him the Insignia of the Companion of Honor. But the Nobel Prize, the most desirable prize of prizes, has eluded him. Those in charge of Nobel require, no, demand "proof" of bold new theories like his. They do not acknowledge, or honor, theories alone. The doctor never made the Nobel cut and his detractors in the highfalutin world of big-time Science, to say nothing of the brash British press, have often referred to him, derogatorily, as "a cult figure."

On occasion, Hawking, more mischievous than saintly, has used the wheelchair's synthesized voice as a remarkable retaliatory measure. At a dinner party for Edward Teller, the so-called "father of the hydrogen bomb," Hawking reportedly caused the synthesizer to bellow, "He is stupid." That got everybody's attention at the table.

In Geneva, at a conference of physicists, the Doctor, seated on the dais, decided to pooh-pooh the speaker's theories on the movements of certain galaxies. With malice aforethought, he made his synthesizer whine and hiss constantly. The audience had trouble hearing what the guy at the mike was saying.

Which suited Hawking just fine.

Understand that the man never explains, never complains, never apologizes. When people annoy him, he has been known to bump, or run over, their toes with his wheel chair. It's rumored that Hawking once knocked against Prince Charles's toes.

What makes his wheelchair a real stunner is that the synthesizer chats in an American accent. You know: The authoritative, but not overpowering, pharmacy voice that tells you what telephone buttons to push when refilling a prescription?

Maybe his voice-choice is a link to his staunchest American admirers: Bill Clinton, Shirley MacLaine, Kevin Costner. His stock retort to those silly enough to question why the Englishman's synthesizer talks in "American," is: If I changed my accent to, say, French, my wife, Jane Wilde, would divorce me.

Actually Jane did, in 1991. It had nothing to do with the synthesizer.

After twenty-six years of marriage, and three children, Jane, whose solicitous character parallels that of Jane Eyre, finally left his "care" to his primary nurse, Elaine.

There were twitters, sizzling gossip, that the doctor and Elaine, a headstrong woman with a mass of flaming red hair and a fiery temper, had enjoyed some sort of romantic encounter. Hmmm.

He married Elaine, and later divorced Elaine, following reports that she had abused him. Police investigations of the allegations (cut lips, black eye, slash marks on the cheek, etc.) were dismissed. However, *Vanity Fair* (June 2004) reported that one day, in desperation, the doctor put the following hysterical "help!" message on his computer: "I cannot be left alone with her. Please don't go. Get someone to cover the shift."

He was referring to Elaine....

Now, Hawking's care is divided between medical professionals and handpicked students who volunteer their spare time to cater to his constant needs. Their pay, readily agreed upon, is having the Doctor give "extra" attention to their papers. He is considered a master at bartering and at negotiating the complicated legal details of his big-deal contracts.

The much-revered, world-famous Hawking is very upper-crust English. He was born in Oxford, is a mathematics professor at Cambridge University and, holds (not literally!), the chair held by Sir Isaac Newton in 1663.

His chalet, reportedly in the $3.6 million-plus range, has a huge sliding glass door that overlooks a sprawling, manicured garden. Weather permitting, that's where the Doctor likes to take his morning coffee.

Hawking's university salary isn't why he's rich.

When he hyped sunglasses and toys on British television, his price was said to be $2 million. His fluky, 1988 science bestseller, *A Brief History of Time*, difficult to read, sold 10 million copies, beating out Madonna's book, *Sex*. Hawking's surprise hit, and subsequent $6 million windfall, has been described as "the most widely unread book in the history of literature."

Every so often, the fabled MacArthur Foundation gifts big-buck awards to lucky recipients chosen very secretly. The Doctor was given a generous MacArthur grant, reportedly administered through Cambridge University, and specified for his care and nurturing.

He has another side, quirky.

He has shown up in Dilbert cartoons, on *Star Trek* and in a skit on *Late Night with Conan O'Brien*, alongside comedian Jim Carrey. Gossip, just gossip, is that the Doctor likes nudie bars. And hearsay has it that he saw a Marilyn Monroe impersonator sing, *I Want to Be Loved By You*, and ordered a photo of the real Marilyn attached to his bathroom door.

Can Hawking actually talk?

A tracheotomy stole his ability to speak in 1985.

But here's the drawback: A normal speech range runs somewhere between 120 and 180 words per minute. One student, the leader among Hawking's groupies, told me that he manages *ten* words a minute on the voice synthesizer. I'd read somewhere that a "switch" clipped to his glasses got his synthesizer talking. I know nothing about the magical technology of the man's talking wheelchair. So please don't ask.

What I did know then, upon learning that the doctor's answers would be excruciatingly slow, was that my interview questions would have to be fast, fast. There wasn't a second to waste.

I did not ask questions about quantum physics. I did not ask about the two scientific theories he'd punched into our American jargon (phrases sometimes used pornographically): "The Big Bang" concept that the universe suddenly exploded into being 15 billion years ago, or "The Black Hole," an outer space place that has so much gravity that nothing escapes from it, not even light.

I asked Hawking if he had hope, even when there didn't seem to be any.

It was as if Mt. Vesuvius had erupted again.

The Doctor was surrounded by a bevy of anxious students, who fluttered around him like the flocks of pigeons that rule the entrances to Milan's old cathedrals.

They froze, in flight, when the "hope" question was posed. The doctor's cold eyes probed, registered disapproval, shot me dark shadows of suspicion.

Everyone seemed to stop dead in their tracks. The synthesizer was stuck on silent.

I filled in the awful gap. I said that hope infuses us with power, energy, opens up new channels of courage. It fuels ambition. His disease ruined his body. But his brain, his most magnificent asset, remained intact. Hope, I said, is a blessing.

Do you have hope?

A half-smile flickered across his face.

The synthesizer ignored the word "hope." It zeroed in on the word "courage." It said:

"I get embarrassed when people say I have courage. It is not as if I have had a choice and have chosen the more difficult alternative. I have simply followed the only course open to me."

Are you afraid to die?

"I am not afraid of death. I have lived with the prospect of an early death for much of my life. But I am in no hurry to die. I still have a lot I want to do. I think death is like the breaking down of a computer. No one has suggested an afterlife for a computer."

The doctor paused, searched my face for a clue that I'd gotten his subtle joke about dead computers. Planned obsolescence, I said straight facedly, like people. He grinned.

Synthesizer: "A sense of humor is important. The world would be a pretty awful place if one took it seriously."

Do you think you've been lucky in terms of fame?

Synthesizer: "I have been very lucky. My condition has not affected my ability to do what I've always wanted to do: physics. I have been lucky to get more help than most people in my position. So I have not needed so much determination. It is the less fortunate who have to be determined to keep going."

Parties. You like parties.

Synthesizer: "I don't enjoy parties much unless they are with people I know. It is difficult, with strangers, to be more than one of the wonders of modern technology with my computer system. The reaction of strangers to my system is generally: 'Ooooh! Aaaah!'"

Do you think a lot about your situation, dwell on it?

Synthesizer: "It's true my illness has given me time to think. But I'm afraid that much of it is about physics, and that is boring. The rest I like to keep private."

The man is extremely intuitive. He sensed that I was inching into the realm of "personal." I had questions about his then-wife, Jane, and how they coped with a life dominated by his devastating disease. He stopped me in my tracks.

Synthesizer: "I am not bitter. I might have been bitter if I had been less fortunate. But I have been successful in my work. I have a beautiful family, and I have written a bestseller. One can't hope for much more."

There's a flip side to the doctor's personality. *Vanity Fair* quoted the Doctor as saying: "No one can resist the idea of a crippled genius."

I'd heard variations of that quote before. I didn't repeat it. Instead, I said: You've been quoted as saying that your physical situation has enhanced your success.

The synthesizer popped up: "That's a misquote. My illness has not helped my career."

A moment of thoughtful silence, before the synthesizer admitted. "But it has not been too serious a handicap."

I think your disease is a handicap and….

The synthesizer pipes up: "It prevents me from doing some things – like writing and equations. It has the compensation of keeping me off committees and involvement in undergraduate teaching."

That elusive, low-key English humor again.

Do you believe in God?

Synthesizer: "Like Einstein, I don't believe in a personal God. I study the beginning of the universe because I want to know where we came from. I think this interest in our origin is shared by most people."

Do you think you have a great imagination?

Synthesizer: "I don't think I have more imagination than many people. It's just that I can concentrate my imagination on physics."

Do you think of time as your enemy?

"I always feel I am in a race against time, like I am now. But I think it has nothing to do with my condition. It's just that I have more things to do than time to do them. I'm glad it's not the other way around. I have to go now."

The Doctor meant he had to "go" as in use the toilet. He has no control over the basic functions of his broken-down body. One of his students rolled him to into the bathroom, stayed with him, and rolled him back.

"Goodbye! Goodbye!" was how the Doctor dismissed me when he crossed the bathroom threshold. I have regrets about this interview. He, and his entourage, thought I'd gotten too close, asked too many emotionally-charged questions.

I wanted more.

You've heard me say that before. Journalists always want more. Their need for more is insatiable.

Everyone has sad milestones that mark turning points in their lives — indelible incidents that never disappear. Stephen Hawking's devastating disease is an enormous burden. Even now, at retirement age, he seeks further fame, lasting fame, perhaps as a substitute, or balance, for the cruelties heaped on him, early, by schoolyard bullies.

When he was at St. Albans, an English boys' school with military leanings, he met up with schoolyard bullies, cruel ruffians, who dubbed him "The Monkey."

He was never a handsome boy.

The boys also bet each other bags of candy that Hawking

would "never amount to anything" there, in school, in their midst, or anywhere else, then or in the future.

Sometimes people in the Doctor's position get the last laugh.

One of the four buildings of St. Albans is named after him. The Monkey turned out to be the world-famous Dr. Stephen Hawking, a man heralded as the greatest scientist of our time. Sometimes he returns to St. Albans to speak, and to be interviewed by the current editor of the student newspaper, *The Albanian.*

I left the Doctor, thinking: I'll bet he gives the boys at school more interview time than he did to me, a she.

Billy Crystal

On kidding around...

It's funny where a dream can start –
that's what it's all about
-Jerry Stiller, actor, comedian

What put me on red alert was finding myself in the claws of that classic *cliché*, the one that made headlines when Princess Di announced, on international television, "Three's a crowd."

It happened to me one dawn at the Hotel Plaza Athenee, in New York, the city that never sleeps, at an early-early breakfast interview with Billy Crystal, my Famous Man of the Hour.

The huge hotel restaurant, a sea of tables primped with crisp white linen and fine white china, was totally deserted except for: (1) Billy Crystal, (2) Crystal's manager, totally unexpected, a blank-faced man wrapped tightly in a new London Fog trench coat, and (3) me.

What made the threesome crunch even worse is that Crystal had reserved a choice banquette. He motioned for me to slide in first, a gentleman's gesture, which made my left shoulder brush the wall. Crystal slid next to me and directed the Trench Coat man to sit on his right.

So there we were. Three little ducks lined up in a neat little row.

Trench Coat, whose name was not announced in-introduction, nodded briefly. It was the nod of exclusion. He and Crystal immediately fell into a two-way conversation, clinching a business deal, leaving me stranded, out of the loop, shoved aside.

The trio had become a duo.

There was no way to flee the banquette without creating a fuss. I'd been trumped. I wasn't the woman journalist sitting next to the wall. I was the fly on the wall.

So here's the specific problem:

Trench Coat had snagged the identical appointment hour that I thought was mine. Same day. Same time. Same place. I didn't know if Crystal was trying to dodge me or if his office made a scheduling error.

Alas, for whatever reason, no interview was in progress. Crystal gave his agent top priority. Why not? They were jibber-jabbering about projects that would make millions. Our values were poles apart. That became especially clear when Crystal turned his face to the right and his agent turned his face to the left – a pose that put the two men in a cheek-to-cheek huddle.

Only the waiter dared to interrupt them. And only for a moment.

The two men quickly ordered full-fledged, man-sized breakfasts. A pitcher of orange juice. Eggs Benedict. Warm croissants. Unsalted sweet butter. A basket of gourmet jams and jellies.

A large pot of fine, aromatic coffee arrived pronto, before the food, piping hot, just like Dunkin' Donuts offers now. I opted only for a cup of coffee, black.

While the waiter served, Trench Coat held Billy Crystal in his sway.

Okay, this is like playing cards. I'd been dealt a low hand, not unusual in the annals of a woman journalist temporarily jumping into the life of a famous man.

As I sat there, talking to myself, I remembered Theodore Roosevelt's theory, the one that put him in the White House: Do what you can, with what you have, where you are.

Okay, said my muse to me: Billy Crystal must be a discriminating person, a good judge of people. He isn't going to leave you dead in the water. Give Crystal the benefit of a doubt. What may look like a storm brewing might be a passing cloud.

Okay, I'm playing poker in my mind, hoping my cards will ultimately be better suited than Trench Coat's hand. But this is a high-stakes game. The "pot" we're playing for, this Trench Coat man and me, is Crystal's attention. I've got to bluff myself back into the interview

I wanted the Billy Crystal interview that Billy Crystal didn't want to give me. I wanted to end up with the most chips. Maybe he's just kidding around.

That's what I was telling myself.

Stranded, trying to figure a way out of this mess, I couldn't help overhearing what the boys were saying to each other in conspiratorial whispers. A newspaper person is usually not privy to such insider information.

How much? Crystal asked.

Mr. Trench Coat cupped his hands around Crystal's ear and uttered the offer very softly.

"Not enough!" Crystal balked.

Then the numbers were spoken openly, in single digits, only I knew they meant six zeroes.

Trench Coat referred to the man in charge of the "dough" (dollar dough – this was not a piece of cake!) as a "currency bastard." Crystal didn't like that. The hand he extended toward the coffee pot stopped in mid-air became a fist, ready to punch. But Crystal is a born kidder. He pursed his lips. Wiggled them back and forth. Then he wiggled his nose. He said he had an idea.

"Yeah?" Trench Coat asked.

"Maybe I'll do less work for the same dough," Crystal smirked.

Trench Coat said he'd put Crystal's deal on the table.

And I'm thinking: if Crystal lets me eavesdrop on this farce, this chat with his collusive cohort, maybe he thinks I'm a journalist to whom he'd like to talk. I mean: I really shouldn't be here, stuck in the corner, privy to this exchange.

Maybe Crystal trusts me. On the other hand, maybe I'm being naïve.

Trench Coat veered the conversation to his client's upcoming bookings. He didn't talk cities. That would reveal too much. He used the names of entertainment palaces. Well, buster, I know a reference to Las Vegas when I hear it. When Trench Coat was chewing his Canadian bacon, I tested the waters, asked Crystal a warm-up question:

Is it true that you hate going to black-tie events because some fool rushes up to you and asks: "How do I look?"

Mischievously, his eyes twinkling, he looked straight ahead, not at me, and said: "They all expect me to say 'mahvelous.'"

Are comics really like clowns, laughing on the outside, crying on the inside?

"I can't be 'on' all the time. That would be boring," Crystal said, nibbling a corner of a croissant. "But people expect me to be 'on' even when I'm offstage. People expect too much of a comedian. No matter what, you're always expected to be funny. I resent that. I'm basically shy...."

The quote begged expansion, one question opening up another question. Billy Crystal is not a shy man.

"Shy" suggests timidity.

The situation we were in had been orchestrated by a bold person, a man who more or less does what he wants, an independent.

Suddenly, the business meeting was over. Finished.

Trench Coat left hastily, no acknowledgement of me. I was not going to cash in my meager remaining chips and skulk home. Billy Crystal, who'd already paid the bill, didn't move. I couldn't move unless he moved. Crystal turned around and, for the first time, we were in face-to-face close-up.

Crystal stared. It was the stare of introspection.

He was deciding what to do with me.

You owe me this interview, I insisted. I'm playing poker, taking chances with my meager cards.

Crystal must have thought I was a rookie, someone who'd accept rejection, dismissal, without a fair fight. He smiled. I smiled. He said, hold on, he'd reschedule the interview. All it would take was a telephone call. He got no further.

No! I said, more vehemently than necessary.

"Why 'no!'" was Crystal's comeback. His imitation of me sounded comical.

I told him he owed me the interview, now. It sounded like an ultimatum. Men hate ultimatums. On top of everything, all Crystal had to do is walk away. Famous men, like all men, do that when the woman sounds authoritative. I fully expected to be ditched.

"Not now!" Crystal said.

I thought he was a goner and, as far as my newspaper was concerned, so was I.

But halleluiah! He rattled off a specific time, later in the day, promising it would be my slot, reserved time especially for me, explained that he was staying there, at the Plaza Athenee.

I didn't even know if I believed the guy.

On a beautiful white linen napkin he scribbled his room number with a black ballpoint pen. He slammed the napkin in my palm as if it were a disposable Post-It and disappeared.

He could have been setting me up, again.

Journalists are, by nature, cautious. I marched to the concierge desk.

Is Billy Crystal staying here? The concierge looked at me as if I was nuts.

I pointed to the number written on the napkin. Is this Billy Crystal's actual room number? The haughty concierge glanced at the beautiful napkin gone graffiti. He set his mouth in a straight line and gave me a look of combined disapproval and snootiness.

He said zilch.

I slipped him a $20 bill, a mandatory, out-of-pocket expense. The concierge checked the dollar value, sneakily, so his cohorts wouldn't see the bribe amount, and quickly replied: "Oui!"

Editors frown on such frivolous expenditures. What do they know about crucial interview tactics? I never put the bribe on my travel voucher.

The damaged napkin? Extraneous. I left it there, propped on the concierge's counter, but only after I'd written Crystal's room number in my notes. Then I ran to a telephone booth and started rearranging my appointments to accommodate Billy Crystal's change of schedule.

All day, a scared feeling gnawed at me. It wouldn't be so marvelous if Billy Crystal stood me up again. We hadn't gotten off to a very good start. Maybe he thought of me as a practical joke. Maybe....

Not only was the man in his hotel room at the appointed time, he'd left the door ajar. Neither a knock nor a buzzer was necessary. I knocked anyway. He strode toward me, hand extended, his funny face bathed in a smile of good will.

What I liked is that he never let on that he'd actually checked out of the hotel. I found this out later. He'd tacked time for me on the end of his busy schedule.

Nice.

Another thing I learned about Bill Crystal: He's not the wise ass he sometimes appears to be onstage. He's a sensitive man, more vulnerable than you might guess. He's more like Harry, as in *When Harry Met Sally*, a good guy.

The courage of your convictions.

Crystal brought up the subject, surprising for a comedian.

What makes people dare to face serious consequences by taking non-traditional actions? He asked me what I thought. This was my interview, not his, and since I didn't know how much time he was going to give me, I took charge.

I asked Crystal if he had a hero who personified that kind of independence, someone who took the road less traveled, and took a beating. His answer was wonderful:

"The great hero of my life is Muhammad Ali. From him I learned it's never too late to start over. He had the courage of his convictions. In 1966, he said: 'I'm not fighting in a war.' He bucked the system. He was stripped of his passport.

"Some people stand up for a cause. Ali believed in himself. So he stood up for himself. I think each person should think of himself or herself as a cause. If you don't fight for yourself, no one will fight for you."

I wondered if, in a roundabout way, he was talking about me.

I'd fought for the interview after the morning shut-out. But, ultimately, he let me win.

Crystal said he was familiar with the bitter taste of rejection, how you fall into a depression, think less of yourself, weaken your sense of self esteem.

"I got cancelled in 1992 by NBC, *The Billy Crystal Hour*, after two shows. I thought negatively. I said to myself: 'You've blown it. That's it. You're done.' I was hard on myself. Finally, after a few months, I said: 'I've got to make my cause myself.'

"I knew the only way to continue was to start over. And I did. Some people think success is the same as getting an Academy Award. I think success is getting to the point where you can say 'no' to projects you know are wrong for you."

Crystal stumbled over the word "no." He'd almost said "no" to the interview and to me.

The two words I hate most are "no" and "you can't."

I grew up in the "no" atmosphere and, by virtue of The Force upstairs, reached the point where I was sitting around the Plaza Athenee having a great conversation with Billy Crystal.

I told him that the world is full of strugglers, people who are hungry to make a mark, so they take on any reasonable job to keep going. You, Billy Crystal, can say "no" because you're a star. You have the pick of the litter.

"I don't think of myself as a star," he objected. "And when I hear the word 'superstar,' I go crazy. I've never liked super savings or super sales. It sounds so phony. I've always wanted to be accepted as me."

Hey, it's because you are who you are that I rearranged my schedule today. If your name was Joe Bloke, I'd be on another assignment or, better, I'd be on my way home.

The word "home" struck a chord. Home is where Crystal's talent was born, where he gathered his first audience, where he began to exaggerate into comedy the family scenes bustling around him.

These are his spoken, boyish memories. They beam the nostalgia of beginnings.

"Sometimes I feel I'm back in my living room, a kid standing on the coffee table, mimicking my relatives. I was nine years old. I was the family's stand-up comic.

"The brunt of my jokes was Uncle Mac. He always struck me as funny. I'm one of three brothers. He certainly knew my name. But, on purpose, Uncle Mac called me by one of my brother's names (Joel or Richard). He wanted me to think he was confused about my identity.

"My mom was the wardrobe mistress. The relatives came and piled their coats on my bed. So I went to the 'wardrobe,' got Uncle Mac's coat, put it on, hopped up on the coffee table in my living room and, addressing Uncle Mac directly, called him my brothers name. I got laughs. And dimes.

"Uncle Mac and his wife had terrible arguments in the car. I rode a lot with them. Sitting in the back seat, I absorbed their fights. They loved each other. But they had ferocious arguments. It was always about who was sicker. They fought about life without a gall bladder versus life with migraine headaches...."

I giggled. Crystal was talking seriously. But the whole thing was so funny.

"My uncle Mac would say, 'Remember the time I had a 104-degree fever?' Then my aunt would say: '104 degrees? That's not a fever!' By the time I was eight, I did exaggerated impersonations of their fights. Laughs. I always got laughs."

Why are you drawn to laughter?

"Early on, I knew that laughter felt good. Now I know the truth is that while you're laughing, you're thinking positively. My father always told me: 'Do what you feel you really want to do.' He died when I was fifteen. Suddenly, he wasn't there. But, in my mind, I know he would be happy for me today, just as he was when I was a kid, acting up."

Is there a link between positive thinking and success?

"Success makes you positive. I'm more positive than I ever was. The things you wanted to happen actually happen...and you feel that anything's possible. But there's a negative side to success. You get criticized."

You've already explained how much you hate rejection. Criticism is a form of rejection. When I said that, Crystal scowled.

"Not long ago, I got a bad review (for *Running Scared*). I let the review spoil my day. But then I went to a movie house and saw people were lined up waiting to buy tickets to the movie. And, I said to myself: 'How silly you are to get upset over trivia.'"

This morning, when we, ahem, talked, you used your tag word, "marvelous." Where does it come from?

He said he saw actor Fernando Lamas on *The Tonight Show* and, with his accent, he pronounced the word marvelous as "mahvelous."

Crystal is an artist, an originator, a creator who snatched the word and built it into a signature. All greats are exhibitionists. It's their facilitator. Their instrument.

"So I began fooling around with Fernando's voice, imitating him. I telephoned my manager."

I interrupted. You mean the Trench Coat man with whom you had breakfast instead of giving me my interview?

"Yup," Crystal said, red faced.

But he quickly picked up his story with aplomb. He took a gimmick, used it as a crutch, made the word his. He spoke in a torrent about how "mahvelous" was born.

"I telephoned my manager, and his secretary said: 'Who's calling?' And I said: 'Ferrr-nanndo-Laaa-Mas.'"

At first, the hoax went undetected.

"My manager thought I really was Fernando Lamas.

"So he says to me: 'And how's Esther?' (That was Esther Williams, the movie-star swimmer, Lamas's wife at the time.)

"I said: 'Mahvelous!'

"'And how's Lorenzo?' (Lamas's son).

"I said: 'Mahvelous!'

"Every time he asked me about somebody Lamas knew, I said, 'Mahvelous!'"

Then Trench Coat got the joke. It was Billy, his client, on the line, pretending to be Fernando Lamas.

"Mahvelous!" Trench Coat deadpanned into the receiver.

Crystal was invited to appear on *Saturday Night Live*. He did an unforgettable "mahvelous" skit. Every time he was asked a question, he repeated that foolish contraption of a word, "mahvelous!" It stuck like glue in the public arena – especially when he appeared to be at a loss for words, paused, and for the umpteenth time said: "You look mahvelous."

"The response was incredible. The audience went wild. After that, I used the phrase even more."

People everywhere copied Crystal's phrase. Still do.

Crystal is like all commanding comedians who, like the best cartoonists, exaggerate the personalities, traits, of other famous people and cast their own spell on the character.

Why do you do that? I asked.

"I like to mime people who are totally themselves. I've become Grace Jones. I've become Tina Turner. I've always wanted shock value. I wanted people thinking I was different and, above all, courageous."

Courage. We've come full circle, back to the subject of, "courage," the word that launched the meeting that almost never happened.

I knew this was it, the farewell, but Billy Crystal put it in an original context. He said he wished, right then, that he was on a baseball field, hitting a few balls.

We went down the elevator together. Crossed the reception area together. The concierge, you know the one I mean, pretended not to see us. We left the hotel together. It was late in the day, getting dark.

Crystal's limo is waiting, black and shiny. The chauffeur spotted Crystal, jumped out, opened the rear door, and bowed. Crystal hopped in, swallowed by the moveable cavern, that long car with tinted windows.

I couldn't see him. But he wanted me to see him. He hit a button. The window closest to him vanished into the down slot.

Before the sleek Caddy pushed toward heavy Park Avenue traffic, he stuck his hand out of the open window, waved, and said "Bye, Mahvelous!"

Afterword

People often ask a question that stumps me.

"Who was your favorite interview?"

There is no "favorite" in the sense of finding one famous person I've loved forever at first sight, some pedestaled legend whom I thought was a perfect person, someone who endeared himself, or herself, to me in an unforgettable way – and in sixty minutes or less.

Nope.

My favorite interviews were the ones where famous people said the unsaid, spoke their innermost thoughts – even when I had to dig, or pull them out — knowing it would be printed. Whether or not I liked them is inconsequential.

My other favorites were famous people who did or said outrageous things, were flamboyant or nutty but, big but, who didn't shoo me away, kept me in the loop, all the while making fools of themselves.

Bad interviews can be good, as in interesting, because I witnessed madness firsthand, not from a darkened movie theatre, or at a Broadway show or on reality television. These famous people were funky, foolish, funny in my face. When my interview turned into a full-fledged circus, the show was my show, for better or worse.

I've already told you about Lord Snowdon's stupid guessing game. It was so bad it was good. So was Anthony Quinn's backward approach.

Even more ridiculous, more gaudy and gross, was Salvador Dali, the Spanish surrealist artist who was a surreal maniac.

His most famous painting is called *Persistence of Memory*, a canvas depicting a weirdly desolate place where a series of watches are in the process of melting. Dali respected neither time nor the clocks that reminded him of time.

Call it first-hand knowledge.

I spent two dull, draggy hours (will-he-come-or-will-he-not?) waiting for Dali to show up at the King Cole Bar, in the St. Regis Hotel, New York City. I'd placed several semi-frantic calls to his publicist, who assured me, calmly, that the man "was on his way."

Dali didn't have a long commute.

He lived upstairs, in a luxurious suite, along with a hysterical Russian wife, Gala, and, it was rumored, a pet ocelot. His vehicle of transportation was the elevator. His other vehicle-of-note was the S.S. Norway, the Norwegian Cruise Line, stateroom No. V139, which welcomed the Dali couple and their beautiful wildcat with the zig-zag stripes.

Dali and I had a 10 o'clock appointment.

It was high noon when the art messiah arrived.

I heard a forceful, rhythmic, bang-bang-bang coming my way. I thought, first, a mafia hit man had made his presence known somewhere in the immediate vicinity of the nearby revolving door.

It was Dali, dressed like a flamboyant old gypsy, black satin *toreador* pants tucked into heavy boots, with heels thick enough to hammer out flamenco rhythms as he danced-pranced his way to my table.

Dali was a small man. But he had amazingly strong feet. The sounds he moved to weren't muffled by the nice wall-to-wall carpeting.

Dali flicked his long cape, florescent fuchsia, expertly over the heads of startled guests sitting, sipping, at small tables that led to mine. New Yorkers are immune to extreme exhibitionism, normal everyday sidewalk sightings, but they seemed stunned that the strange whooshing sounds made by Dali's cape came close enough to dislocate certain important coiffures.

This scene happened under the watchful gaze of a huge, Maxwell Parrish mural of King Cole, displeasure written on his face, his band of merry old souls taking it all in, like me.

All human eyes were on the madman. He sported his familiar handlebar moustache, heavily waxed, and he'd smeared a thick mask of Max Factor pancake makeup on his face. Layered on his cheekbones were uneven splotches of red rouge. His turquoise eyelids sported pasted-on, false lashes that looked like spiders. His lips were the color purple.

It seemed safe to assume that, while I waited downstairs for two hours, this buffoon was upstairs preparing himself for the interview.

What was truly comical was that Dali was still sporting small, old-fashioned, metal hairdresser clips clamped to two still-damp spit curls, one sitting above each ear. He'd forgotten to remove them. The rumor was that Gala, his ill-tempered Russian wife, spat on Dali frequently, especially when they had spats.

Perhaps those spit curls were of Gala's doing.

The tuxedoed Bar manager didn't drop the arm pointing me out until Dali reached my side. Like this abominable distraction was all my fault.

Dali, his hair dyed jet black (or was it a wig?), made a loud proclamation. First he looked at me, then he looked at the gaping gazers and announced:

"I vant sumzing for sumzing. I do nuzzing for nuzzing!"

(Translation: I want something for something. I do nothing for nothing.)

What he wanted was money, to be paid for the interview. Dali said he would not sit down, or talk, unless he got money then and there. My newspaper did not, probably still doesn't, pay for interviews.

This was extortion. A holdup. I had to think faster than a Pentium-4 computer. Dali, the lunatic genius who ruled the international art world, had mesmerized the hotel guests. Of course, money is inconsequential until you need it.

No piles of $20 bills for Dali. I reached for my wallet and retrieved a penny.

I put the penny on the table, looked the madman in the eye, and told him a white lie. I assured Dali that the penny was very, very dear to me. It was my lucky penny. It was very painful for me to part with the coin because it was a family heirloom, a gift from my dead mother. It was, I said, a good-luck coin. Anybody who possessed it was guaranteed good luck.

It's yours.

Dali sat down opposite me.

The penny was a dirty old useless coin. Dali, high on something, put it between his teeth as if he planned to chew it. He ingested many germs that day. He smelled it as if it were expensive perfume and said, "Ahhh!"

Dirty old pennies don't smell nice. He put it to his ear as if it were a seashell complete with echoes. He held it up to the ceiling light to see if it was transparent.

Certifiable, I thought.

We talked. I don't remember about what.

What I do remember is that he laughed at things that weren't funny, a hyena's laugh, high and piercing. Dali was not capable of answering sensible questions and delivering excellent quotes.

He was, at that moment, merely a flamboyant-famous artist who seemed to be driven by demons. I wished that he was in a condition to speak of those demons, identify them, tell me how they affected him, as if I already didn't know.

There was no possibility of uncovering his inner truths. He was not in his right senses.

What he showed me, this living picture of himself, gussied up like a gypsy, painted up like a lunatic, was more melodramatic than any words he might have spoken.

Salvador Dali was, in fact, one of my favorite "interviews" because he told me much about his state of mind without telling me a thing.

The Author

Marian Christy is the author of the critically acclaimed books *Letters from Legends and the Incredible Interviews that Inspired Them, Famous Women Speak Out* and *Invasions of Privacy.*

During her twenty-six year tenure as a *Boston Globe* syndicated columnist and editor, she was the recipient of thirty prestigious national and international journalism awards(1965-1991). She made journalism his-

tory when she became the first and only three-time winner of the highly coveted University of Missouri School of Journalism's J.C. Penney Award (1966, 1968, 1970).

Following an early retirement from *The Boston Globe*, she was the head writer and host of The Monitor Channel's *Lifestyles With Marian Christy* cable television program.

Christy became a frequent contributor to The New York Times Syndicate and, in 1998, was made the first media director of Boston University's Special Collections, assigned to negotiate and host black-tie press events, such as honoring Prince Albert of Monaco and Hollywood superstar Meryl Streep.

Christy joined *The Globe* as fashion editor in 1965 after a distinguished career with New York-based Fairchild Publications, writing major features for *Women's Wear Daily*. Her first

Boston Globe assignments were in Europe, where her prize-winning editorials emanated from the major *couture* salons in Paris, Rome, Madrid, Barcelona, Athens, Dublin and London.

Christy completed elective studies at Harvard University's Extension School, and earned a journalism certificate from Boston University in 1965. She was awarded a Distinguished Alumni Award for standards of excellence in journalism from Boston University's College of Communications in 1985. Her papers, manuscripts and letters are collected at Boston University's Howard Gotlieb Archival Research Center.

In October 2003, Crane & Company, international paper makers, featured a month-long exhibit of fifty letters, many handwritten, to Christy by celebrities. Many of these appear in this book.

In 1987, she received an Honorary Doctorate of Humane Letters from Franklin Pierce College, Rindge, New Hampshire.

Christy switched to celebrity journalism in 1981 and single-handedly created the original "Conversations" column format, oral history based on revealing, one-on-one talks with highly achieved people from a wide variety of fields. Christy's pioneering work — recording in a newspaper format the great voices of our time — has resulted in her being called "the literary Oprah Winfrey." Coral Lansbury, the late dean of women at Rutgers University, referred to Christy as "the Boswell of our times."

Marian Christy is quoted extensively in numerous books, including...

The Last Editor (Jim Bellows)
Claus Von Bulow (William Wright)
Joan: The Reluctant Kennedy (Lester David)
Pat Nixon: The Untold Story (Julie Nixon Eisenhower)
My Father and I (Camelia Anwar Sadat)
Snowdon (David Sinclair)
The Kirkpatrick Mission (Alan Gerson)
Interviews with Betty Friedan (Janann Sherman)